Amazon Sellers' Guide:

Chinese Intellectual Property Law

Table of Contents:

Introduction

Purpose of the Book:

This book focuses on informing Amazon Sellers about protecting their brand from threats located in China and steps Sellers can take to prohibit infringers. We discuss trademark and copyright law, the two primary ways to protect your brand around the world.

Firm Profile:

Rosenbaum Famularo, P.C., focuses on the needs of Online Sellers. We have lawyers, paralegals, former online sellers, and others on staff around the world. Our clients have the opportunity to meet with us, in person, at locations in New York, Shenzhen, Yiwu and Melbourne.

Online Sellers are not alone anymore.

Rosenbaum Famularo, P.C., the law firm behind AmazonSellersLawyer.com has obtained the reinstatement of countless Amazon Sellers' accounts and listings. The firm has obtained retractions of complaints from numerous brands and resolved many issues with Amazon's staff in the United States, India, Ireland, Costa Rica, and the United Kingdom.

The partners of the firm, CJ Rosenbaum and Anthony Famularo regularly speak at events for Sellers around the world.

Rosenbaum Famularo's other books include:

- *Amazon Law Library, Volume 1*
- *Your Guide to Amazon Suspensions*
- *Your Guide to Selling Fashion on Amazon*
- *Amazon Sellers' Guide: Trademark Law*

Rosenbaum Famularo provides more free content for Amazon Sellers than any other company or law firm. If you want to learn more about Intellectual Property law for e-commerce Sellers, please visit one of our following social media accounts:

- Instagram: @RosenbaumFamularo
- ASL Twitter: @AmazonSellerLaw
- RF Twitter: @Merchprotection
- YouTube Channel: Rosenbaum Famularo, P.C.
- Facebook: Amazon Sellers' Lawyer
- Websites: amazonsellerslawyer.com and rosenbaumfamularo.com
- Google Plus: Rosenbaum Famularo
- LinkedIn: Rosenbaum Famularo
- Reddit: Amazon Sellers Lawyer (u/Rosenbaum Famularo)

Since starting my practice in 1994, I have represented entrepreneurs who operate both online and brick & mortar businesses. I am also a courtroom lawyer and litigator. I have represented people across the United States, have taken countless depositions, and tried more cases each year than most lawyers do during their entire careers.

I have successfully litigated cases against some of the largest corporations in the world, including: McDonald's, Sears, Kentucky Fried Chicken, and many insurance companies.

- In NYC, I have successfully obtained redress for my clients against the NYPD, the NYC Housing Department, the NYC Health and Hospitals Corp., and other behemoths.
- I have represented clients in the internet, finance, health and entertainment industries.
- I have been admitted to practice law in state and federal courts.
- I hold executive and leadership roles in the NYS Bar Association and the National American Association for Justice.
- I have delivered lectures to other lawyers in New York, Chicago, Montreal, Maryland, Florida and California.

Authors

CJ Rosenbaum, Esq.

CJ is the founder of the firm. He is known around the world for teaching tens of thousands of Amazon Sellers how to avoid suspensions. CJ teaches Amazon Sellers how to get their accounts back efficiently is they suffer a suspension of their Amazon Sellers' Account or the loss of the ability to sell one or more specific products. CJ has published thousands of pages of free guidance for Amazon Sellers. CJ started focusing on helping Amazon Sellers years ago after learning that Amazon Sellers needed someone that could analyze accounts, draft concise and persuasive Plans of Action, address intellectual property issues and also represent Amazon Sellers against Amazon at arbitrations when Amazon refuses to amicably resolve issues. CJ uses his extensive prior education and experience in business and business law, negotiations, law for entrepreneurs and his fifteen years as a trial lawyer to help Amazon Sellers.

Prior to CJ, there was seemingly nobody who understood what was needed to win an arbitration and was then able to use that information to analyze accounts and draft persuasive Plans of Action. Fast forward to today, CJ, and his partner, Anthony Famularo, are responsible for saving thousands of Amazon Sellers' Accounts, thousands of businesses and likely tens of thousands of jobs around the world.

As Amazon Sellers pivoted into developing their own Private Label Brands, CJ, Anthony and the entire team at Rosenbaum Famularo, P.C., grew to help Private Label Sellers. The number one firm for helping Amazon Sellers is also the number one firm to help Sellers as they develop, monitor and protect their brands and their intellectual property rights.

Having written the books on selling on Amazon, CJ, Anthony and their firm law are uniquely qualified to help Sellers protect their intellectual property rights.

Anthony Famularo

Anthony is the Managing Partner at Rosenbaum Famularo, P.C. Anthony has worked with CJ from the beginning of the focus on Amazon Sellers. Anthony's experience includes addressing tens of thousands of issues related to Amazon and other e-commerce Sellers and intellectual property issues.

After working with CJ and saving countless accounts and jobs across the United States as the New York Managing Attorney, Anthony was made a Partner of the firm in 2016.

Anthony manages a team of over twenty lawyers, paralegals and support staff around the world.

Anthony has written or edited more Plans of Action than anyone in the world.

Conor Wiggins

Conor is the Manager of the Legal Research and Writing Team at Rosenbaum Famularo, P.C. He is pursuing his Juris Doctor at the Maurice A. Deane School of Law at Hofstra University and will graduate in 2019 with a concentration in Intellectual Property Law.

In addition to his work with Rosenbaum Famularo, P.C., Conor is the student Editor-in-Chief of Volume 44 of the American College of Trust and Estate Counsel Law Journal. His strong legal writing skills and passion for Intellectual Property law allow him to run an effective team and best serve our client's legal needs.

Moshe Allweiss

Moshe is a second year Law Student at Maurice A. Deane School of Law at Hofstra University, working as a summer associate at Rosenbaum Famularo, P.C. Law Firm. He graduated from Queens College undergrad with a bachelor's degree in applied physics as well as honors in history. He hopes to utilize his physics degree to pursue a legal career focused in patent law.

At Hofstra University, Moshe works for the Law, Logic and Technology Lab alongside a team from Carnegie Mellon and the University of Pittsburg, the team that helped invent IBM's "Watson," to assist U.S. Veterans. When Moshe is not studying or working, he enjoys singing, writing parodies, and making board games.

Editor

Adina Grodsky

Adina is a 2021 Juris Doctorate candidate at the New England School of Law in Boston. She holds a Bachelor of Arts degree in Political Science, and a minor in Chinese language.

Illustrator

Dave Kopka

Dave is a Brooklyn-based artist and graphic designer. He is the illustrator for the entire *Sellers' Guide to* series with Rosenbaum Famularo, P.C.

- Email: illustration@davekopka.com.
- Website: davekopka.com.

Chapter 1: Then and Now: A Brief History of Intellectual Property in China

Introduction

Anyone interested in understanding intellectual property in China need only do a quick Google search to realize that the Chinese intellectual property landscape is tumultuous. President Trump's 2018 tariffs called for a "big fine"[1] over Chinese-treatment of U.S. intellectual property law and for an end to the "greatest transfer of wealth in history,"[2] at over $600 billion a year in lost intellectual property profits[3]. Chinese-handling of American intellectual property seems to be one of the few bipartisan issues remaining in the U.S. However, this view of Chinese intellectual property, from a purely-American lens gives China more undue criticism than the country deserves.

The Chinese marketplace is booming and ripe for investment. The breakneck development of e-commerce companies like Amazon, Alibaba, and eBay have provided the keys to the global marketplace not just for corporations, but also individual Sellers to market their products

---

[1] Jeff Mason, *Exclusive: Trump Considers Big 'Fine' Over China Intellectual Property Theft*, Reuters (Jan. 17, 2018), https://www.reuters.com/article/us-usa-trump-trade-exclusive/exclusive-trump-considers-big-fine-over-china-intellectual-property-theft-idUSKBN1F62SR.
[2] Dennis C. Blair and Keith Alexander, *China's Intellectual Property Theft Must Stop*, NY Times (Aug. 15, 2017), https://www.nytimes.com/2017/08/15/opinion/china-us-intellectual-property-trump.html.
[3] *Id.*

all over the world. As such, it is absolutely paramount that Sellers understand their intellectual property rights in China.

The seeming lawlessness of intellectual property in China has often garnered it the title of being a "wild west." However, China's intellectual property law is just one small component of China's ancient and storied history. While China continues to update, improve, and standardize their intellectual property rights, it is important for Sellers to understand that with a history as long and as notable as China's there are bound to be cultural and societal differences that influence exactly *what* intellectual property *means* to the Chinese people. Therefore, before delving into the specifics of registering for and protecting intellectual property rights in China, we must first understand where intellectual property rights have *come from* in China. China's long-standing history of intellectual property can be divided into three distinct phases: Ancient China, Maoist China, and Post-Mao China.[4]

---

[4] Staff Editor, *China's Long and Tortured History When It Comes To Intellectual Property Laws*, JIPEL Blog – NYU Journal of Intellectual Property & Entertainment Law (Feb. 4, 2014), https://blog.jipel.law.nyu.edu/2014/02/chinas-long-and-tortured-history-when-it-comes-to-intellectual-property-laws/.

(I). China's Historical and Cultural Interpretation of Intellectual Property Rights

(A) Ancient China

Intellectual Property is nothing new in China. China's first copyright regulation was announced by the Emperor in 835 A.D. This original copyright regulation prohibited artistic works portraying natural events from being created since it was understood at the time that the Emperor was the link between the people and occurrences in the natural world. Trademarks began to develop during the Tang Dynasty (618-907 A.D.) when traders began using marks and logs to distinguish their goods from others.[5] This later flourished into a system during the Ming Dynasty (1368-1644 A.D.) which allowed manufacturers to register trademarks with other guilds.[6]

The ideals of Confucianism are often noted as a counter to this early intellectual property development in China. This philosophy valued the importance of the community over the individual, and it is well known that Confucius had a disdain for commerce and working solely for profit.[7] In complete opposition to this philosophy, Western capitalism and the utilitarian interpretation of intellectual property rights

---

[5] Hamideh Ramjerdi & Anthony D'Amato, *The Intellectual Property Rights Laws of The People's Republic of China*, 21 N.C.J. Int'l L. & Com. Reg. 169, 172 (1995).
[6] Charles Baum, *Trade Sanctions and the Rule of Law: Lessons from China*, Stan. J. E. Asian Aff. 46, 51 (2001), http://www.stanford.edu/group/sjeaa/journal/china4.pdf.
[7] Wang Lewei, *The Chinese Traditions Inimical to Patent Law*, 14 NW. J. Int'l & Bus. 15, 36-56(1993).

grant "limited monopolies"[8] to those who possess them. In response, others have argued that Confucianism protects individual rights differently from the West by creating a culture where personal Development and innovation is extremely important but for the good of the community rather than the individual.[9]

---

[8] *China's Long and Tortured History*, JIPEL Blog (Feb. 4, 2014), https://blog.jipel.law.nyu.edu/2014/02/chinas-long-and-tortured-history-when-it-comes-to-intellectual-property-laws/.

[9] Wei Shei, *Cultural Perplexity in Intellectual Property: Is Stealing a Book an Elegant Offense*, 32 N.C.J. Int'l L. & Com. Reg. 1 (2006); *quoting* John R. Allison & Lianlian Lin, *The Evolution of Chinese Attitudes toward Property Rights Invention and Discovery*, 20 U. Pa. J. Int'l Econ. L. 735, 744 (1999).

(B) Maoist China

It is widely recognized that intellectual property ceased to exist in Maoist China. The Cultural Revolution brought about by Mao and his communist regime oversaw the complete elimination of the concepts of both physical and intellectual property. The copyright laws of the 1950's in China actually *prevented* Chinese publishers from paying or seeking permission from foreign rights-holders to use their works unless they were from another socialist nation.[10]

(C) Post-Maoist China

Shortly after Mao Zedong's death, the Chinese intellectual property landscape again began to change drastically. In 1979, China signed a bilateral agreement with the United States recognizing and allowing for the protection of American copyrights, trademarks, and patents, in China.[11] Throughout the 1980's, China became party to many international bodies and treaties such as the World Intellectual Property Organization, the Berne Convention, the Paris Convention, and the Patent Cooperation Treaty.[12]

---

[10] *China's Long and Tortured History*, JIPEL Blog (Feb. 4, 2014), https://blog.jipel.law.nyu.edu/2014/02/chinas-long-and-tortured-history-when-it-comes-to-intellectual-property-laws/.
[11] Qiao Dexi *A Survey Of Intellectual Property Issues In China-U.S. Trade Negotiations Under The Special 301 Provisions*, Pacific Rim Law & Policy Journal Vol. 2 No. 2, 259, 260.
[12] *China Laws (302 texts)*, WIPO World Intellectual Property Organization (last visited Jun. 18, 2018), http://www.wipo.int/wipolex/en/profile.jsp?code=cn.

In 2000, the U.S. China Relations Act's signing normalized trade relations between the U.S. and China and became a permanent installation.[13]

Today, China protects domestic copyrights, trademarks, and patents from the State Intellectual Property Office (SIPO) and the Chinese Trademark Office (CTMO). Under the auspices of these new departments, the People's Court of China received, accepted, and closed 766,101 intellectual property right cases of first impression from 1985-2016.[14] China is outpacing the entire world in both patent and trademark registration. In fact, in 2016, Chinese companies and individuals lead the globe in intellectual property protection registration: 6,997,600 trademarks and 3,127,900 patents were filed.[15] By comparison, and in a very distant second, the United States registered 517,297 trademarks and 589,410 patents.[16]

With all of this historical development in mind, it should be said that instead of criticizing China for conducting intellectual property dispute resolution differently, it is more important to understand the differences in how the U.S. and China handle these issues in order to

---

[13] *U.S. Relations With China 1949-2018,* cfr.org (last visited Jun. 18, 2018), https://www.cfr.org/timeline/us-relations-china.
[14] Supreme People's Court, *China's Intellectual Property Judicial Protection Program (2016-2020),* law-lib.com (last visited Jun. 18, 2018), http://www.law-lib.com/law/law_view.asp?id=566119.
[15] WIPO World Intellectual Property Organization, *China Tops Patent, Trademark, Design Filings in 2016* (Dec. 6, 2017),
http://www.wipo.int/pressroom/en/articles/2017/article_0013.html.
[16] *Id.*

work side by side. From copyright edicts instituted by the Emperor, reinterpretations by the hand of Confucianism, total bans by Mao, and a reunion through international agreements, China has tackled intellectual property issues for thousands of years.

CJ's Side Note: Like everything in the news or on the internet, you need to take it all with a grain of salt. Yes, China has their fair share of intellectual property problems, but all hope is not lost. By having a better understanding of the history of intellectual property law in China, a nation of inventors and innovators, it seems reasonable to assume that intellectual property protections will continue to improve. There has been a positive trend in the People's Court for improved rights and protections for injured parties that have had their intellectual property stolen.

(II). Realities of Chinese Intellectual Property Today

Despite China's long history with intellectual property, it is impossible to deny that protecting intellectual property rights in China today is a real issue. The country remains on the 2017 "priority watch list" of the U.S. Trade Representatives Office's annual "shame list" of countries with poor intellectual property protections.[17] As of November 8, 2017, over 1,600 American intellectual property rights infringements have been uncovered, with countless others yet to be discovered.[18]

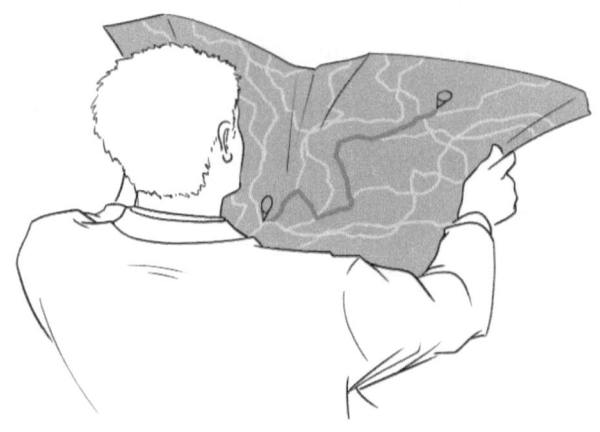

[17] Office of the United States Trade Representative, 2017 Special 301 Report (last visited Mar. 25, 2017),
https://ustr.gov/sites/default/files/301/2017%20Special%20301%20Report%20FINAL.PDF.
[18] *China Uncovers Almost 1,600 U.S.-Related Intellectual Property Infringements This Year*, Reuters (Nov. 8, 2017), https://www.reuters.com/article/us-china-u-s-intellectual-property/china-uncovers-almost-1600-u-s-related-intellectual-property-infringements-this-year-idUSKBN1D90A0.

The question is how does a Seller interested in diving into the Chinese market through global e-commerce ensure that their intellectual property rights are protected? The answer to that question is multi-faceted and at times highly complex.

The first step of this process is to **BE AWARE THAT YOU NEED PROTECTION**.

Chapter 2: Understanding Your Intellectual Property Rights in China

Introduction

The World Intellectual Property Organization ("WIPO"), defines "intellectual property" as "creations of the minds such as inventions; literary and artistic works; designs; and symbols, names and images used in commerce."[19]

The phrase "intellectual property," first and foremost, is an umbrella-term for copyright, trademark, patent, trade dress and trade secret.

This chapter's goal is to provide basic explanations of these rights as they pertain to Sellers and introduce any distinct definitional differences that these rights may have in China when compared to the international community under the WIPO or in the United States.

(I). What Is A Copyright?

Copyright protection in the United States is derived from Article I Section 8 of the U.S. Constitution which grants Congress the power to "promote the progress of science and useful arts, by securing for limited times to authors and inventors the exclusive right to their respective

---

[19] WIPO World Intellectual Property Organization, (last visited Jun. 19, 2018), http://www.wipo.int/about-ip/en/.

writings and discoveries."[20] In essence, copyright protection grants the "author" the exclusive-right to use their copyright to their economic benefit and no one else's without that author's permission to do so. In the United States, copyright protection, for any work created after January 1, 1978, lasts for the lifetime of the author plus an additional 70 years.[21] In China, copyright protection lasts for the lifetime of the author plus fifty years.[22]

Copyright protection in China may be granted by filing a domestic-Chinese application in accordance with the Copyright Law of the People's Republic of China. Alternatively, protection in China may be obtained for a work "published outside the territory of the People's Republic of China which is eligible to enjoy copyright under an agreement concluded between the country to which the foreigner belongs and China, or under an international treaty to which both countries are parties."[23]

> **CJ's Side Note:** There will be more on the details on the several different ways of *how to* apply for copyright protection in China. For now, however, it is only important to understand that there are multiple ways to gain copyright protections.

---

[20] U.S. Const. art. I, § 8.

[21] COPYRIGHT LAW OF THE UNITED STATES, ch. 3, § 301(a), (Dec. 2016).

[22] COPYRIGHT LAW OF THE PEOPLE'S REPUBLIC OF CHINA, art. 21, § 3 (Feb. 26, 2010).

[23] *Id.* art. 2.

Under Chinese copyright law, copyright protection extends to "works of literature, art, natural science, social science, engineering technology and the like which are expressed in the following forms:

1. Written works;
2. Oral works;
3. Musical, dramatic, quyi', choreographic and acrobatic works;
4. Works of fine art and architecture;
5. Photographic works;
6. Cinematographic works and works created by virtue of an analogous method of film production;
7. Drawings of engineering designs, and product designs; maps, sketches and other graphic works and model works;
8. Computer software;
9. Other works as provided for in laws and administrative regulations."[24]

As is clear from this list, copyright protections in China extend to a wide array of works: from writings to computer software, from videos to architecture.

(II). What Is A Trademark?

A trademark is "any word, name, symbol, or design or any combination thereof, used in commerce to identify and distinguish the goods of one manufacturer or seller from those of another and to indicate the source of the goods"[25]. A trademark signifies for the

---

[24] COPYRIGHT LAW OF THE PEOPLE'S REPUBLIC OF CHINA, art. 3.
[25] 15 U.S.C. § 1127.

consumer that the product he or she is purchasing will deliver the same consistent quality that has been associated with that good.

China is the most robust market for trademark applications in the world. In 2016, 3.691 million trademark applications were filed by Chinese people and companies.[26]

> **Anthony's Breakdown**: The Nike swoosh, the stylized way the Hewlett-Packard Company (HP) writes "hp," and the Starbucks mermaid are all examples of valid trademarks. As soon as you see any of these symbols or lettering, you know the exact source of the product you are buying and already have an expectation for the product's quality based on that brand's goodwill and reputation.

While there are a vast array of words, names, and symbols that can be registered for trademark protection, many things cannot be registered. Generic words and pictures of items that naturally grow or exist in nature are not eligible for trademark protection.[27]

---

[26] AFD China Intellectual Property Law Office, *China's Trademark Application Amounts to 3.691 Million in 2016* (Mar. 2017), https://www.lexology.com/library/detail.aspx?g=e81f8156-da99-435f-8cdc-5ee6fbe6865f.

[27] CJ Rosenbaum, *Your Guide to Amazon Suspensions*, 45 (2017-2018 ed.).

There is little definitional difference in China, as opposed to in the United States or internationally, as to what a trademark *is*. One distinct difference, however, is that the Chinese Trademark Office (CTMO) does not require applicants to prove that they are using their mark at the time of application.[28]

China allows companies to register their trademark for multiple classes of trademark regardless of whether they ever intend to use the trademark in that way. This system is called "first-to-file" and is one of the issues which may confront a seller entering the Chinese market.

The "first to file" system can be advantageous to prepared Sellers or corporation. One such foreign company that has taken advantage of this in China is Starbucks, which has registered their STARBUCKS trademark in all 45 classes of Chinese-trademarks under the CTMO.[29]

(III). What Is A Patent?

Patents protect novel and non-obvious inventions and technological processes. Patents are registered in China through S.I.P.O.

---

[28] Matthew Dresden, *China Trademarks, The Madrid System, And Star Trek*, China Law Blog (Jul. 10, 2016), https://www.chinalawblog.com/2016/07/china-trademarks-the-madrid-system-and-star-trek.html.
[29] *Id.*

(State Intellectual Property Office of the People's Republic of China), which governs all patentable material in China.[30]

China is the international hub of patent filings. In 2016, there were more patent applications in China than in the United States, Japan, the Republic of Korea, and the European Patent Office *combined*.[31]

When a party wins a patent-infringement claim, they may be able to recover 100% of all the profits made by the sale of that product.[32] A 100% recovery can be devastating to even the largest companies.

(IV). What Is Trade Dress?

In the United States, trade dress protects the "overall appearance" of the product so long as the trade dress is both "inherently distinctive" and the alleged-copier's trade dress is "likely to cause consumer confusion."[33] Trade Dress protects a product's and a color schemes, packaging, and other aspects of the product.

In China, there is no specific law of trade dress. In China, trade dress can be protected under copyright law, trademark law, patent law,

---

[30] State Intellectual Property Office, SIPO.gov (last visited Jun. 19, 18), http://english.sipo.gov.cn/.

[31] WIPO World Intellectual Property Organization, *China Tops Patent, Trademark, Design Filings in 2016* (Dec. 6, 2017), http://www.wipo.int/pressroom/en/articles/2017/article_0013.html.

[32] CJ Rosenbaum, *Your Guide to Amazon Suspensions*, 52 (2017-2018 ed.).

[33] Trade Dress, law.cornell.edu (last visited Jun. 19, 2018), https://www.law.cornell.edu/wex/trade_dress.

and unfair competition law.[34] While there is no specific trade dress law, because this protection can be invoked under all different fields of Chinese intellectual property, it makes trade dress a potential avenue for a Seller to protect their products and their appearance. This defensive tactic will be elaborated on further in chapter seven.

---

[34] Xuri Bao, *China: Strengthening Trade Dress Protection In China*, World Trademark Review (May 01, 2017), http://www.worldtrademarkreview.com/Magazine/Issue/67/Country-correspondents/Strengthening-trade-dress-protection-in-China.

(V). What Are Trade Secrets?

A trade secret is a form of intellectual property protection that protects against others from using information that is valuable because it is not known in the trade. To qualify, the information has to be secret and the information holder must continuously take reasonable measures to keep the secret.[35]

Trade Secret law generally protects what the lay person would consider to be a "secret recipe," or whatever makes a product unique and one-of-a-kind and gives it a competitive edge in that marketplace (i.e. Inventions, designs, ingredients, algorithms).

Anthony's Breakdown: Coca-Cola's recipe, the criteria for the New York Times Bestseller list, Google's search algorithm, Twinkies' ingredients are all examples of famous trade secret protections.

Trade Secret theft is a significant problem in China. In 2011, an employee of a Massachusetts-based wind turbine company that had begun doing business in China was arrested and sentenced to a year in prison for selling the "crown jewel" trade secrets of the company for an

---

[35] Ran Wang and Xiaojing Wang, *Protecting Trade Secrets In China*, Managing Intellectual Property (Sept. 06, 2017), http://www.managingip.com/Article/3748735/Protecting-trade-secrets-in-China.html.

offer of $2 million, women, apartments, and a new life in China.[36] Stories like this are not uncommon in China. Sellers should be very protective of their trade secrets.

Similar to Trade Dress, there is no specific Trade Secret law in China. A Seller can, however, gain Trade Secret protection under Article 10 Section 3 of Unfair Competition Law. Article 10 prohibits business owners from infringing upon trade secrets by: stealing, luring, intimidation or any other unfair means.[37] As a result, knowledge of what secrets are important to a Seller's products, and the means by which to protect these secrets, makes the protection of trade secret another important component of any Seller's intellectual property protections.

Conclusion

Intellectual Property is a blanket term for a wide array of protections that a Seller can obtain to protect themselves from potential infringers of their products. The first step in a Seller equipping themselves with a bundle of intellectual property protections is understanding all the different types of protections, what they are and what they protect.

---

[36] Clare Sebastian, *Chinese Trade Secret Theft Nearly Killed Company,* CNN tech (Mar. 23, 2018), http://money.cnn.com/2018/03/23/technology/business/american-semiconductor-china-trade/index.html.
[37] LAW OF THE PEOPLE'S REPUBLIC OF CHINA AGAINST UNFAIR COMPETITION, art. 10, § 3 (Dec. 1, 1993).

Chapter 3: Registering Your Intellectual Property in China: Preventing Issues Before They Occur

<u>Introduction</u>

Savvy Sellers will register their products in China because **if a seller does not file their copyrights, trademarks, or patents in China, that Seller has no formal intellectual property protection in China.**[38]

This chapter's goals are twofold:

(1) Provide Sellers with a basic explanation regarding which IP rights they can register in China, and;

---

[38] *Best Practices: Intellectual Property Protection in China,* The US-China Business Council (2015), https://www.uschina.org/reports/best-practices-intellectual-property-protection-china.

(2) Provide Sellers with a basic understanding of how to preempt the most common issues that occur during the

registration of their intellectual property rights in China.

(I). Registering for Copyright Protection in China

A Seller, technically speaking, does not need to register their copyright because China is a member of the Berne Convention[39] which

---

[39] *WIPO-Administered Treaties*, WIPO World Intellectual Property Organization (last visited Jun. 19, 2018),
http://www.wipo.int/treaties/en/ShowResults.jsp?treaty_id=15.

means copyright protection is an automatic right granted to all member-nations of that agreement.

In the event of an infringement of a copyright, however, a Seller with copyright protection derived only from the Berne Convention would have to prove their copyright by submitting the original work(s), translating complicated legalese, and notarizing documents, all from overseas.[40] This process could potentially be very tedious, complicated, and costly. No Seller wants their business interrupted in such a way. Therefore, **the savvy Seller will register his or her copyright in China under Chinese Copyright Law.**

> **Anthony's Breakdown:** Registering for Copyright Protection in China, while not *technically* necessary, should be done as part of your protection plan. It will help to streamline the process of addressing infringers.

The easiest and most cost-effective way for a Seller to protect their products eligible for copyright protection in China is to get a signed

---

[40] *How To File A Copyright Registration In China*, China IPR (2018), http://www.china-iprhelpdesk.eu/sites/china-hd/files/public/v8_How_to_Register_Copyright.pdf.

Certificate of Registration from the Copyright Protection Center of China ("CPCC").[41]

The Chinese registration process is fairly straightforward. The following is a step-by-step process for online application for copyright protection in China.

1. The Seller goes to http://www.ccopyright.com/ (the CPCC's website).
   a. Ccopyright.com is a Chinese-based website. If the Seller is not literate in Chinese, they should seek assistance from one who is; please contact our firm and we can provide the Seller with a translation. *IF* the Seller wishes to proceed on their own, however, the Seller should access the website via google and use the translation link at the top of the page to translate a portion of the site into English.

---

[41] Matthew Dresden, *China Copyright Law: We Need to Talk*, China Law Blog (Oct. 17, 2016), https://www.chinalawblog.com/2016/10/china-copyright-law-we-need-to-talk.html.

2. The Seller sets up an account on the CPCC site. From the main page, the Seller clicks "Copyright Registration" which will bring the Seller to a new page.

---

42 Copyright Protection Center of China (last visited Jun. 19, 2018), http://www.ccopyright.com/.

3. If the Seller does not already have an account, he or she clicks on the link on the right-hand side of the "User Login" module underneath "forgot password?" A new page will appear where the Seller needs to fill out all the relevant information about his or her business.

43

4. The Seller returns to the page from Step 4 and clicks "I want to register." The first link under the "Online business" module.

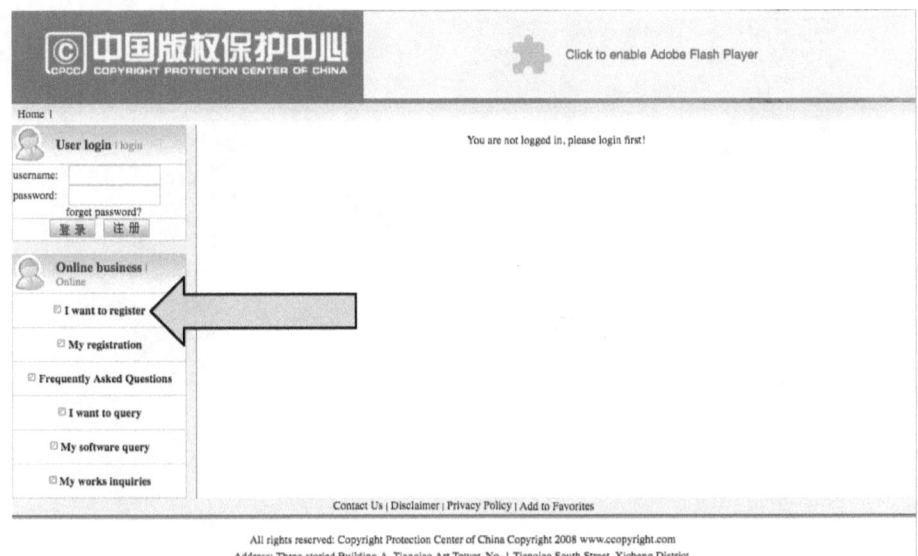

44

5. Depending on the type of copyright protection the Seller is seeking
    (see chapter two for descriptions of what type of protection is being
    sought) the Seller selects either "R11" (the blue arrow) for a
    computer software copyright and fills out the application form that
    drops down or selects "Z11" (the yellow arrow) for an application
    for a work's copyright registration and fills out the application form
    that drops down.

---

[44] *Id.*

Figure 2

45

6. The Seller prints the completed application form and sign/affix his or her seal onto the copy.

7. The Seller posts or hands in the registration files to CPCC

---

[45] *How To File A Copyright Registration In China*, China IPR (2018), http://www.china-iprhelpdesk.eu/sites/china-hd/files/public/v8_How_to_Register_Copyright.pdf.

8. The Seller's files are checked by CPCC. If approved, the Seller may continue to Step 9. If not approved, CPCC will inform the Seller as to the error(s) in the application.

9. The Seller pays the registration fee and receives the "Notification of Receipt of the Application."

10. The Seller's registration will be examined by CPCC. If approved, CPCC will issue the certificate for the newly-approved registration and make an announcement on their website to fulfill the final requirement of "public knowledge."[46]

(A) Preempting Common Copyright Registration Issues

Even after a Seller has properly registered for, and acquired, copyright protections in China, the copyright law of the country allows for twelve exceptions that will *not* violate someone's copyright. Depending on what the Seller is selling online, some of these may be more or less applicable to the individual's situation:

1. Personal use;
2. "Appropriate" quotation in order to introduce, comment on, or explain;
3. Use by the media to report current events;
4. Republishing or rebroadcasting another media source's story;
5. Publishing/broadcasting a public speech;
6. Use as a scientific work for purely teach or research purposes;
7. Use by the government "to a justifiable extent for the purpose of fulfilling its official duties;"
8. Reproduction for public display, such as a museum or library;
9. A free live performance;

---

[46] *Id.*

10. Copying, drawing, photographing or video-recording a public artwork;
11. Translation of a *Chinese citizen's* work from Mandarin to a minority Chinese language, for distribution in China; and
12. Transliteration of a published work into braille for publication.[47]

Sellers need to be aware of these exceptions to copyright protection. These are very *similar* to the American legal-system "Fair Use" exception.

While the *process* of registering for copyright protection is relatively-straightforward, the reality on-the-ground in China is a far different story.

A Seller can have all the proper registration but that will not necessarily stop China's rampant copycat problem. In a recent undertaking by *Slate*, the magazine found that nearly 90% of all DVDs distributed in China were unauthorized copies.[48] Statistics like this are common in China. Sellers should be aware that the country is routinely on the United States Trade Representative ("USTR") "Priority watch

---

[47] COPYRIGHT LAW OF THE PEOPLE'S REPUBLIC OF CHINA, art. 22, § 4 (Feb. 26, 2010).

[48] Christopher Beam, *Bootleg Nation*, Slate (Oct. 22, 2009), http://www.slate.com/articles/news_and_politics/explainer/2009/10/bootleg_nation.html.

list" for common intellectual property infringers.[49] China appeared on this list as recently as the 2017 report.[50]

Despite those realities, copyright protections in China are improving. Sellers should certainly still register their rights in the country.

China's signing of the Berne Convention in 1992[51] was a recognition by the nation that they will meet the same minimum standards as many of the world's other nations:

- Copyright protection shall be for the life of the author plus fifty years after their death.[52]

The 2017 USTR report positively reported that:

- Positive statements by high-level Chinese officials on their goal to strengthen the nation's intellectual property protections;

---

[49] Office of the United States Trade Representative, 2017 Special 301 Report (last visited Mar. 25, 2017), https://ustr.gov/sites/default/files/301/2017%20Special%20301%20Report%20FINAL.PDF.

[50] *Id.*

[51] *WIPO-Administered Treaties*, WIPO World Intellectual Property Organization (last visited Jun. 19, 2018), http://www.wipo.int/treaties/en/ShowResults.jsp?treaty_id=15.

[52] *Id.*

- Increased recognition of trade secrets as a form of intellectual property protection;
- A new law was drafted regarding e-commerce and submitted for review in December of 2016. New rules are expected to become law sometime in 2018.

(II). Registering for Trademark Protection in China

Sellers seeking to protect their trademarks in China have two options: (1) to register under the international agreement the "Madrid Protocol" or (2) to register in China itself with the Chinese Trademark Office ("CTMO").

While both options provide Sellers trademark protection, there are differences regarding filing ease and effectiveness of each method. Generally speaking, registering under the Madrid Protocol is easier while registering with the CTMO may give the Seller an edge in any future trademark disputes that may arise in China.

(A) Trademark Registration Via the Madrid Protocol

The Madrid System is an international agreement that allows persons to register their trademarks under different nation's trademark systems through a single and standardized system. The allure of the Madrid System for the Seller looking to enter the Chinese marketplace is that the **registration process can entirely the easy-to-use English-language WIPO website** at http://www.wipo.int/madrid/en/.

Anthony's Advice: For Sellers with a smaller operation or a non-Chinese speaking Seller, the Madrid Protocol offers a quick and practical alternative to filing trademark applications with the Chinese Trademark Office.

Breakdown of Madrid Protocol Trademark Registration

(1) **Eligibility** - registration under the Madrid Protocol merely requires that the Seller be a citizen of one of the 116 nations covered by the agreement. Checking eligibility should be the first step in the Seller's process to registration.

(2) **Brand Search** - the WIPO website provides a user-friendly tool to search their international database of registered trademarks. The Seller should use this to preempt and prevent any future issues that could arise.

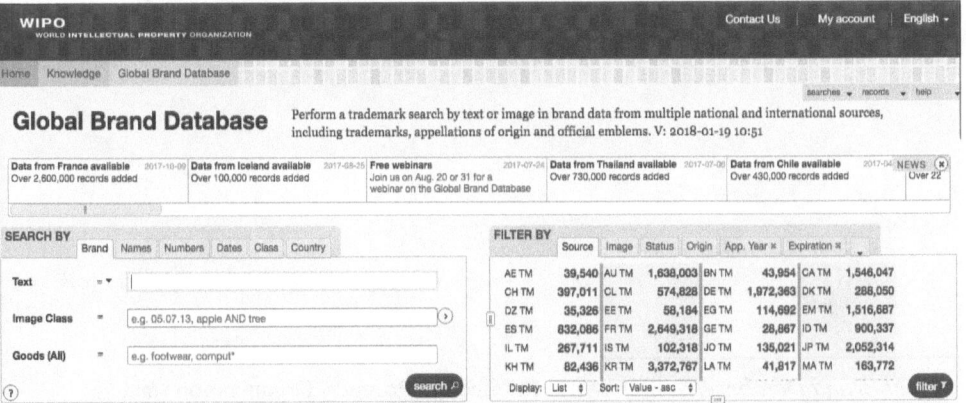

53

(3) Filing - the WIPO website provides a link to the 11-page registration document to file for an international trademark application.

54

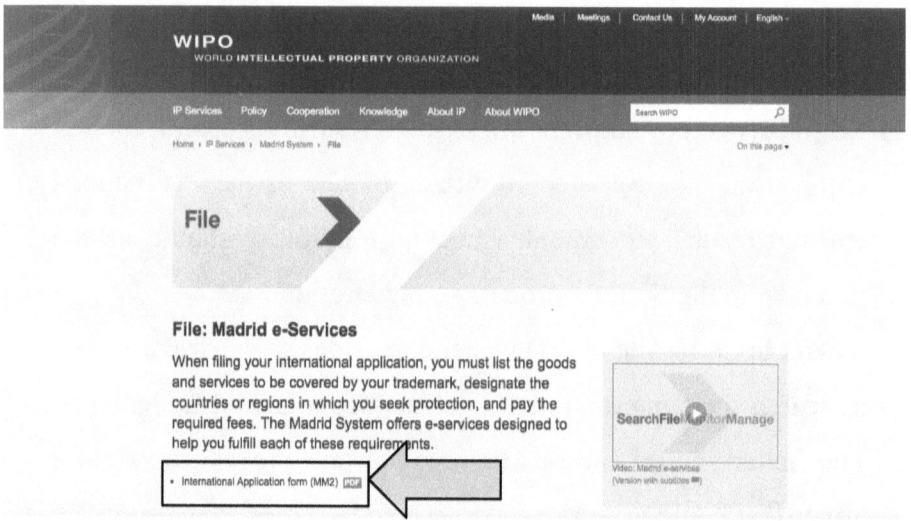

---

[53] *Global Brand Database,* WIPO World Intellectual Property Organization (last visited Jun. 19, 2018), http://www.wipo.int/branddb/en/.

[54] *File: Madrid e-Services,* WIPO World Intellectual Property Organization (last visited Jun. 19, 2018), http://www.wipo.int/madrid/en/file/.

(4) Cost - registration costs 653 Swiss Francs (approx. 679 USD) + country cost + nature of the mark + number of classes registered for. The website features a cost-calculator that a Seller can use even before registration begins to decide whether or not they wish to seek trademark protection.

55

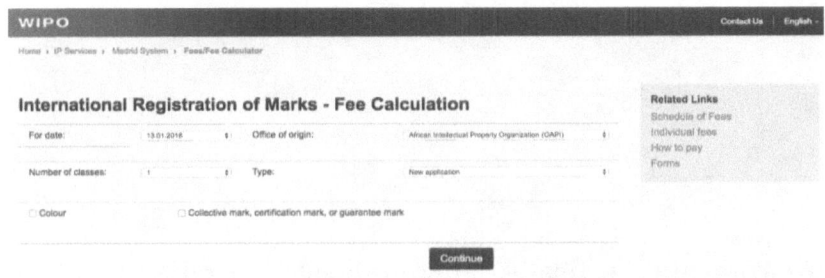

(5) Monitoring - After the trademark application has been filed, the WIPO offers a useful monitoring tool for the Seller to watch their application as it moves along the approval process. It also gives the Seller the ability to monitor other similar trademark applications that may potentially be competing with theirs.

---

[55] *International Registration of Marks – Fee Calculation*, WIPO World Intellectual Property Organization (last visited Jun. 19, 2018), http://www.wipo.int/madrid/en/fees/calculator.jsp.

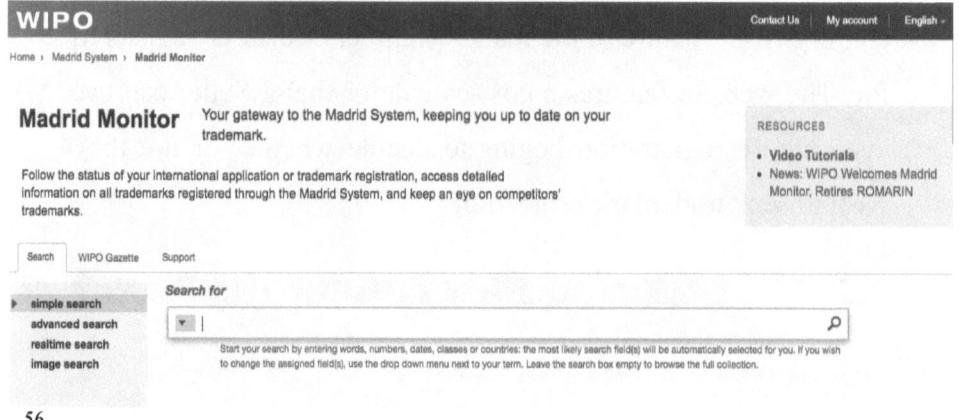

(6) Managing - finally, after a Seller's application has been approved and registered as a trademark, sellers have the ability to monitor their trademark and tailor it with their changing business needs.

Reality of the Madrid Protocol

The Madrid Protocol is a great system but it is by not without its shortcomings. The greatest flaw with choosing to seek protection in China via The Madrid Protocol is that WIPO, rather than the Seller him or herself, files the trademark application with the CTMO. The CTMO then reviews the application for approximately eleven months. During this time, the Seller will have no contact with the CTMO. Therefore, if

---

[56] *Madrid Monitor*, WIPO World Intellectual Property Organization (last visited Jun. 19, 2018), http://www.wipo.int/madrid/monitor/en/index.jsp.

a trademark is not approved by the CTMO, the applicant will learn of the failed application only after, roughly, eleven months. The notice of the failed application will travel from the Chinese CTMO to WIPO and then WIPO to the applicant.

This system leaves the Seller without the ability to correct their application *during* the approval process while their application is with the CTMO. If denied by the CTMO, the Seller's only option is to appeal this decision and file for an application review with the Trademark Review and Adjudication Board ("TRAB").

Additionally, WIPO follows the international classification system for products: 25 International Categories. China has hundreds of sub-categories. If you leave a category out, the presumption in China is against having any rights.

(B) Trademark Registration Via the CTMO Directly

A Seller may choose to register their trademark domestically with the CTMO. While not as "one size fits all" as an application via the Madrid Protocol, registering directly with the CTMO has significant advantages.

(1) Registration via CTMO is faster. Registration via the CTMO renders a decision within nine months of filing.[57] Registration under the Madrid Protocol takes twelve to eighteen months.[58]

(2) Registration via CTMO may be "safer." On top of registration being simply faster with the CTMO, it is also, in a way, more secure. If a seller chooses to file via the Madrid Protocol, "it is not unusual that the CTMO does not input right away into its system the data received from WIPO about international trademark extensions."[59] This means, that an internationally-submitted trademark application could potentially be filed *after* a domestically-submitted trademark application. That domestic application would then be approved, registered, and begun to sell products under that trademark before the WIPO trademark, that was submitted first, had a chance to be registered. Therefore, despite China being a "first to file" district, the domestically-filed application may have the upper hand in a trademark dispute with the international-registrant who submitted their application first.

---

[57] TRADEMARK LAW OF THE PEOPLE'S REPUBLIC OF CHINA, ch. II, art. 24 – ch. III, art. 30.

[58] *Summary of Madrid Agreement Concerning the International*, WIPO World Intellectual Property Organization (last visited Jun. 19, 2018), http://www.wipo.int/treaties/en/registration/madrid/summary_madrid_marks.html.

[59] Wanhuida Peksung, *How to File? Directly in China with the CTMO or Through International Extension to China?*, Wan Hu Dai Intellectual Property Express, No. 32 (Jul. 2016 Issue), http://www.managingip.com/Article/3669018/How-to-file-Directly-in-China-with-the-CTMO-or-through-international-extension-to-China.html..

Additionally, if a Seller files in China's CMTO directly, she can choose all of China's sub-categories that the Seller seeks protection.

> **CJ's Summary**: When you file with the CTMO, your application is both approved more quickly and *filed directly with the source*. Even though a Madrid Protocol application may be simpler, it puts a middleman between sellers and the people reading your application. This gives the people over at the CTMO the opportunity to put internationally-filed applications on the "back burner" for a while; in the world of trademark applications, every second counts. Also, it is better to have proper sub-categories in China. This is especially true in light China's presumption against rights.

Breakdown of a CTMO Trademark Registration

As a warning to the Seller looking to file their application with the CTMO, it is strongly recommended that the Seller seeks legal advice from attorneys experienced in Chinese trademark application. In addition to the application being in Mandarin, a trademark application may be rejected for a series of cultural reasons. Because of that, there are many products that would be approved and many other countries but not in China because of China-specific aversion to such trademarks for cultural reasons.

CJ's Side Note: A Chinese trademark application is equal parts legal jargon and Chinese culture. If you are looking to file for trademark protection in China, we strongly recommend you seek experienced legal help in China.

Trademark law in China is governed by the Chinese Trademark Office. First and foremost, when a Seller is seeking to register their trademark in China they must first determine the "class of goods" that their product is, in accordance with Article 19 of the Trademark Law of the People's Republic of China.[60]

The Chinese trademark office has an extremely wide range of good classifications; thirty-four in total.[61] Some examples of these categories are: chemicals, paints, laundry items, industrial oils, pharmaceutical tools, common metals, machine tools, hand tools, surgical equipment, lighting apparatus, vehicles, firearms, musical instruments, etc. Each category, furthermore, has sub-categories that must be properly selected. A Seller's failure to select the proper classification for their product they are seeking trademark protections

---

[60] TRADEMARK LAW OF THE PEOPLE'S REPUBLIC OF CHINA, ch. II, art. 19 (Aug. 30, 2013).
[61] *Trademark Classifications List of Goods and Services*, Chinese Trademark Office (last visited Jun. 19, 2018),
https://www.chinatrademarkoffice.com/blog/show/190.html.

for can result in an automatic rejection of said trademark or a lack of protection in the sub-categories where no application was filed.

Even after successfully filing a trademark application under the proper goods-category and subcategories, the application process is not over. Those inspecting a trademark application at the CTMO look for any one of the eight possible reasons to reject a trademark application under Article 10 of the Trademark Law of the People's Republic of China. Reasons for rejection of an application are:

1. Identical or similar to a Chinese state name, national symbol, flag, emblem, etc.;
2. Identical or similar to a foreign nation's state name, national symbol, flag, emblem, etc.;
3. Identical or similar to an international bodies' name, national symbol, flag, emblem, etc.;
4. Identical or similar to official signs and hallmarks;
5. Identical or similar to the symbols or names of the Red Cross or the Red Crescent;
6. Those having the nature of discriminating against any nationality;
7. Those having the nature or exaggeration and fraud in the advertised goods;
8. Those detrimental to socialist morals or customs or having other unhealthy influences.[62]

Sections 1-8 of Article 10 clearly give the CTMO a wide range of discretion when analyzing a trademark application.

---

[62] TRADEMARK LAW OF THE PEOPLE'S REPUBLIC OF CHINA, Ch. II, art. 10 (Aug. 30, 2013).

No section gives a wider, and potentially more confusing, range of discretion than section 8, which says that **a trademark may be rejected for having "unhealthy influences" on Chinese society**.[63]

While other nations such as the UK, Germany, and Japan have similar provisions in their trademark laws, none of those nations are socialist countries or steeped in the particularly unique Chinese cultural history. Because of this, it is very easy for a trademark applicant to inadvertently offend socialist or cultural ideals in the eyes of the CTMO.

Furthermore, the CTMO does not need to provide any proof or concrete examples of actually *how* your trademark application would have negatively influenced the people of China.[64] Whether the Seller meant to offend or negatively influence a group of people within China is irrelevant. If the CTMO feels that your trademark application does that in some way, they will reject your trademark application.

> **Anthony's Breakdown**: Section 8 is purposely broad and vague. It allows the CTMO to have the ability to reject your trademark application for a seemingly endless range of reasons, and to do so at their own

---

[63] *Id.*

[64] Wang Ze, Zhou Yunchuan, Zhou Bo, Rui Songyan and Xu Lin, Landmark Trademark Cases in China: An In-Depth Analysis, 61.

discretion with no proof. Practice makes perfect with filing a trademark application; any Seller looking to do this should seek out attorneys both with experience in filing these applications and an understanding of Chinese culture.

If an application is rejected by the CTMO, the applicant has the ability to file an appeal with the Trademark Review Adjudication Board ("TRAB"). This book addresses TRAB appeals in Chapter Five. In essence the applicant must successfully-allege to the board that the objectionable portion of their application won't be realized by the Chinese people.

(III). Registration for Patent Protection in China

First and foremost, **in order to have patent protection in China, the patent application MUST be filed in China.**[65]

The State Intellectual Property Office of the People's Republic of China ("SIPO") is responsible for patent application and approvals. Unlike with copyright or trademark protection, there is no international agreement that can act as an alternative; even if an individual has patent protection under another nation or under an international agreement, the SIPO must still approve the patent for it to be applicable in China.

---

[65] *Guide To Patent Protection In China*, China IPR SME Helpdesk (2013), http://www.china-iprhelpdesk.eu/sites/all/docs/publications/China_IPR_Guide-Guide_to_Patent_Protection_in_China_EN-2013.pdf.

Anthony's Advice: Because the patent application process is so complex and requires a

domestic-application, we highly recommend that a patent applicant seek the help of

attorneys experienced in filing these applications in China.

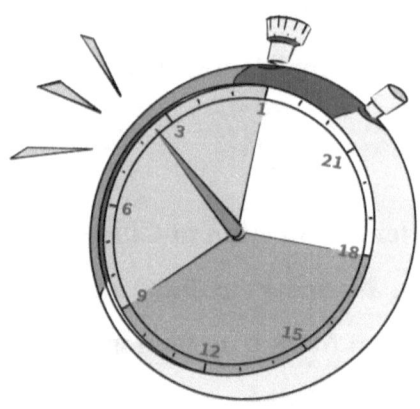

Breakdown of Filing for Patent Protection Under the SIPO

Step 1) Determine What Kind of Patent You Seek

As outlined in chapter two, China recognizes three main types of patents:

1. Invention patents;
2. Utility model patents;
3. Design patents.[66]

This is the first and an extremely crucial step in beginning the patent application process. The protections provided to a design patent, for example, will not provide the type of protections that a registrant will want if what they are actually seeking is an invention patent.

Step 2) Determine How You Will File Your Application

There are three different routes one may take when filing for patent protection in China, they are: (a) Direct Route, (b) Paris Route, and (c) Patent Cooperation Treaty Route.[67]

All three options for registration have their benefits and drawbacks. Each route's merits should be carefully considered before an individual selects their method of patent application.

Direct Route - filing directly in China. If a seller is a foreign national and file directly in China, **you are required to hire a local**

---

[66] Crystal J. Chen, Eric C. K. Hsieh, and Sylvester W. L. Hsieh, China: Managing the IP Lifecycle 2013 *The Patent Application Process Explained*, iam-media (last visited July 16, 2018), http://www.iam-media.com/Intelligence/IP-Lifecycle-China/2013/Articles/The-patent-application-process-explained.

[67] *Guide To Patent Protection In China*, China IPR SME Helpdesk (2013), http://www.china-iprhelpdesk.eu/sites/all/docs/publications/China_IPR_Guide-Guide_to_Patent_Protection_in_China_EN-2013.pdf.

patent agency to handle the filing of the patent.[68] The exception to this rule is that Foreign Investment Enterprises ("FIE") are permitted to apply for patents without a licensed patent attorney.

The benefit to filing directly in China is that there is the lowest chance of your patent application getting "lost in translation." In other words, the SIPO requires all patent applications to be written in Mandarin. If the Seller is a foreign national registering for a patent, he or she will be required to hire a local Chinese patent office. One of the biggest problems with English to Chinese patent applications is that inaccurate translations can lead to rejected applications or patent application challenges further down the road.

The drawback to filing an application directly in China, especially for most non-Chinese readers of this book, is that sellers will have to work remotely with their attorneys.

Paris Route - initially filing a patent in a foreign country and *then* filing the patent in China.[69] The patent applicant may choose this path so long as the nation they first filed the patent application in is a member of the Paris Convention.[70] The Paris Convention has 177

---

[68] *Id.*

[69] *Summary of the Paris Convention for the Protection of Industrial Property (1883)*, WIPO World Intellectual Property Organization (last visited Jun. 22, 2018).

[70] *Id.*

member-nations with the entirety of North America, South America, and Europe as contracting members.[71]

The benefits to the "Paris route" include that previously-filed patents can be transferred over to China and used in the Chinese marketplace. The benefits, however, end there. As previously mentioned, one of the most common issues with patent applications in China comes from errors in translating a patent application in English or another language into Chinese. Furthermore, filing for a patent in this style has strict timeline deadlines that certainly require legal expertise.

Just for example, approval of a utility patent in another country requires a patent application be filed in China within 12 months of *filing* the initial patent; approval of a design patent in another country requires a Chinese-equivalent application be filed only six months after *filing* of the initial patent.[72] These are *very* short deadlines. A filer should certainly have assistance from a patent attorney experienced in Chinese IP law.

Patent Cooperation Treaty Route. The Patent Cooperation Treaty ("PCT") is an international patent treaty agreement with 152

---

[71] *WIPO-Administered Treaties*, WIPO World Intellectual Property Organization (last visited Jun. 19, 2018),
http://www.wipo.int/treaties/en/ShowResults.jsp?treaty_id=15.

[72] *Guide To Patent Protection In China*, China IPR SME Helpdesk (2013),
http://www.china-siprhelpdesk.eu/sites/all/docs/publications/China_IPR_Guide-Guide_to_Patent_Protection_in_China_EN-2013.pdf.

contracting states.[73] This route entails the two-step PCT process: (1) filing an international patent application under the PCT and (2) selecting China as the designation state for registration during the national patent application phase.[74]

There are numerous benefits to the Patent Cooperation Treaty Route. The forms can be filed online in the applicant's native language, and fees are charged electronically through the WIPO.[75] This makes the process simpler, easier, and more cost-effective than either the Direct or Paris Route. Furthermore, after the international phase of the registration process, more than one nation can be selected for the nation phase, potentially allowing the filer to gain patent protection in multiple countries.[76]

Anthony's Advice: Do not be fooled by our surface level explanations overview-explanations of these systems; patent applications can be a very tricky process. Most application routes require an attorney to file the application but even in cases where an attorney is not required it is highly recommended that you retain one. Even if a patent is filed outside of China, the application

---

[73] *Protecting Your Inventions Abroad: Frequently Asked Questions About The Patent Cooperation Treaty (PCT)*, WIPO World Intellectual Property Organization (status on Oct 2017).
[74] *Id.*
[75] *Id.*
[76] *Id.*

will be translated into Chinese. Any imperfections in a translation can doom an application from the start. For a safe, secure, and sound patent, seek legal counsel.

Conclusion

Whether in the United States or China, the best way to solve an intellectual property issue is to prevent the problem before it occurs. Registering for copyright, trademark, and patent protection in the country where a seller wishes to do business is the first-line of defense against infringement claims. Whether through Chinese national offices or international agreements, having a properly-registered copyright, trademark, and patent helps to should be seen as an investment in a sellers' businesses future; these registrations will help to keep a seller's business productive and profitable.

Chapter 4: Copyright: Fighting Infringers and Protecting Your Copyrights

As was covered in chapter two, a seller's "original" work that has gained copyright protection in China is protected for the life of the author (the Seller) plus an additional 70 years after death.[77] While copyright protections last for a substantial amount of time, this certainly does not mean that a Seller in China will not run into any issues with their copyright. There are a significant number of methods Seller can use in China to stop infringers.

(I). Offense: Stopping Copyright Infringers

There are multiple modes of attack a Seller has in their arsenal when addressing an infringer in China. Which method the Seller chooses to use is based upon multiple considerations including:

- how much time the Seller is willing to spend;
- how much money is the Seller willing to spend;
- is the Seller seeking damages;
- how much money has been lost;
- has the infringement risen to a criminal level?

---

[77] COPYRIGHT LAW OF THE PEOPLE'S REPUBLIC OF CHINA, art. 21, § 3 (Feb. 26, 2010).

(A) Contacting the Online Platform

When an internationally-based Seller in China, it is most often discovered when the Seller simply finds their own products being sold on an online-platform such as Amazon, Alibaba, or eBay, without their permission.

When copyright infringement is first discovered, the Seller may seek protection at the border, begin administrative proceedings, file a civil suit, or raise criminal allegations. The Seller should not forget, however, that the easiest and often simplest solution to the problem may be to simply contact the online-platform that is permitting the sale of the products.

At the outset, addressing the issue via the platform is by far the least expensive route to alleviate infringement issues. Many websites, such as Amazon, have pre-established avenues called "take down" mechanisms. When Sellers are successful in employing the platform's take down system, they are able to stop the ongoing infringement. Take Down mechanisms to not provide the infringed party any damages for lost sales or brand degradation.

The downside to contacting the digital sales platform, however, is that it may be no more than a bandage on a far larger wound. A website removing an infringing listing does nothing to prevent that individual from selling on another site or selling via her own website or via brick & mortar stores.

Anthony's Advice: Despite the drawbacks, contacting the online platform selling the infringing-product should be part of a Seller's overall solution. An online platform should be able to take down the infringing product from their site which, at the very least, will at least mitigate the losses you the Seller are experiencing from this infringer stealing your product. From there, the Seller can take further and more-serious action which this chapter will cover.

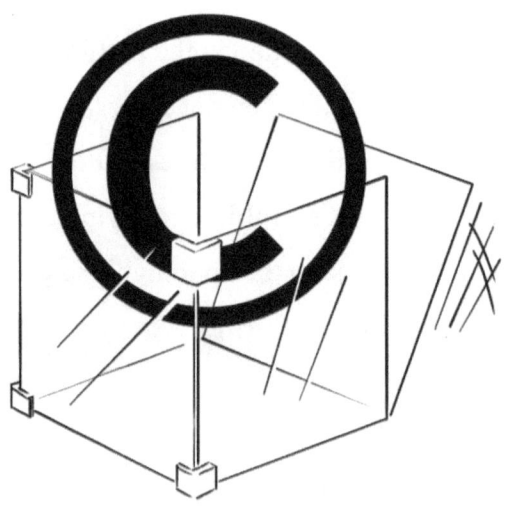

(B) Border Protection

If a Seller's issues with copyright infringement are coming from their products flowing across the Chinese border, either in or out, without their permission, then protecting copyrights via the Chinese border may be a potential solution.

The State Council of the People's Republic of China gives customs the power to seize and protect different items via the Regulations on Customs Protection of Intellectual Property Rights.[78]

Article 2 states:

Customs protection of intellectual property rights used in these Regulations refers to the protection provided by Customs for the exclusive rights to use a trademark, copyrights and their related rights, and patent rights...related to import or export goods and protected under the laws and administrative regulations of the People's Republic of China.[79]

Article 2 empowers China's border protection agents to seize any goods that they believe is infringing upon the Seller's properly-registered copyright protections. This is, however, the limit of the power of customs enforcement to protect Sellers' copyright protection. No damages may be issued by customs nor can they go after the infringer

---

[78] Regulations on Customs Protection of Intellectual Property Rights, Decree No. 395 of State Council of the People's Republic of China (effective Mar. 1, 2004).
[79] *Id.* art. 2.

in the country itself, since their power ends at what comes across the border.[80]

(C) Administrative Proceedings

There are benefits to employing Chinese administrative proceedings as a means of stopping copyright infringers. An administrative proceeding is when the Seller contacts one of the local-level government offices to stop copyright infringers that are infringing in their districts. This local-level work helps to attack specific areas of infringement and can be a much quicker and less costly procedure than going through the court system to stop infringers. Furthermore, if the city-level administrative office administers a decision that is averse to the Seller, the Seller may appeal the decision to the higher province-level administrative board for review.[81]

> **Anthony's Advice**: Be advised, however, that the province's administrative office will not be reviewing the merits of your case. Rather, they will analyze whether the lower-level office properly reviewed your case.

---

[80] *About Customs Enforcement of Intellectual Property Right (IPR)*, General Administration of Customs People's Republic of China (Nov. 18, 2014), http://english.customs.gov.cn/Statics/aafe7743-c701-4795-91e3-6f3fdf7ce397.html.
[81] *Roadmap for Intellectual Property Protection in China*, EU-China IPR2, 16.

Filing a complaint at an administrative office to begin proceedings on the Sellers copyright infringement action is relatively straightforward. The Seller needs to go to the city-level administrative office where the infringement has taken place and bring evidence such as: a copyright ownership certificate, a Chinese recordal certificate, original/draft of the product, a copy of the infringing works, and a purchase receipt of where the Seller can buy these infringing items.[82]

While administrative proceedings can be done more quickly and cheaply than legal proceedings and can be done at the local-level and appealed to higher offices, there are a significant number of drawbacks to this method.

First and foremost, administrative offices cannot issue damages.[83] In addition, because proceedings must begin at the local-level, fluency in Chinese will be needed. This method of redress also seems to require some ability to work the Chinese government.

Similar to other methods that stop the continuing sales, sales, administrative offices lack the power to order anyone to pay damages for prior infringement.[84] In other words, administrative offices cannot stop infringers until a judgement is reached. During the entire investigation and, if the Seller appeals a decision, the appeal process,

---

[82] *Id.* at 17.
[83] *Id.*
[84] *Id.* at 17.

the infringer may still be able to sell these illicit goods without any hindrance.

(D) Judicial Protection - Civil

There are benefits to bringing a civil action in the People's Court against an infringer such as the court's ability to issue preliminary injunctions, to preserve evidence of the infringement and to issue damages.[85] Before a case can be brought, the Seller must demonstrate that their copyright is an original work.

There are multiple levels within the People's Court: Basic, High, Intermediate, and Supreme. Each level consists of different chambers: civil, administrative and criminal.[86] Internationally-based Sellers, such as in the U.S. and U.K., will likely have their matters heard in the Intermediate Courts.[87]

A benefit of employing China's civil judicial system is that the court may impose a preliminary injunction. This is a power that web platforms, customs, or administrative offices cannot offer sellers. A preliminary injunction provides immediate relief to the Seller because it halts all infringing activity until the issues are resolved. Preliminary injunctions can be difficult to obtain and costly. The Seller is often required to post monetary bond estimated at the gross revenue lost by

---

[85] *Id.* at 14-15.
[86] *Id.* at 14.
[87] *Id.* at 15.

the infringer during the injunction-period. The bond will be used to reimburse the infringer if the case is lost – if the infringer is found not to have infringed upon the plaintiff's intellectual property rights.[88]

Another benefit of a civil action is that the court has the power to preserve infringing materials for examination.[89] This is another power that solely exists in the court system. Administrative actions, remedies via customs and or complaints asserted on sales platforms do not result in preservation orders.

A third benefit to a civil action, and likely the most important to the Seller, is that the People's Court has the power to award damages. Not only can the court award damages, but there is also technically no limit to the amount the court may award. As China's overall concern with intellectual property issues have increased, so have the damage-payments; a sign of good things to come for sellers seeking justice in the People's Court.[90]

(E) Judicial Protection - Criminal

Criminal courts in China, like the civil courts, have powers attractive to Sellers seeking justice such as the ability to issue preliminary injunctions, to preserve infringing materials, and to issue damage awards. In addition to these powers, the criminal courts may

---

[88] *Id.* at 14.
[89] *Id.*
[90] *Id.* at 15.

also issue criminal sanctions such as additional fines and incarcerate infringers.

Before a Seller can raise a civil claim to a criminal level, the Seller must prove that the infringement rises to a criminal level. This level is dictated by Article 217 of the Criminal Law of the People's Republic of China.[91] The categories of sales that apply to criminal infringement suits are those infringers who:

(1) copy and distribute written, musical, movie, televised, and video works; computer software; and other works without the permission of their copywriters;

(2) publish books whose copyrights are exclusively owned by others;

(3) duplicate and distribute audiovisual works without the permission of their producers;

(4) produce and sell artistic works bearing fake signatures of others.[92]

The infringements can neither be done accidentally nor a small-amount. The Seller must also prove that the infringer had "knowledge"[93]

---

[91] CRIMINAL LAW OF THE PEOPLE'S REPUBLIC OF CHINA, art. 217, § 7 (Mar. 14, 1997).
[92] Id.
[93] Id. at art. 217.

of his or her infringement and that he or she "gain[ed] a huge amount of illicit income" from the sales.[94]

> **CJ's Side Note:** The evidence must be brought before the People's Court or to the Public Security Bureau *before* the discovery process. Meaning, the Seller must have gathered this evidence on their own or with the help of an attorney before the Seller has the legal-access to all the infringers documentation. This makes bringing a criminal suit that-much-more difficult for the Seller when attempting to bring a civil action.

---

[94] *Id.*

If a Seller can meet the threshold requirements before the court, the Seller may be able to inflict the most serious punishments against the infringer. Besides preliminary injunctions during trial and damage payments at the conclusion, an infringer may be "sentenced to not less than three years and not more than seven years of fixed-term imprisonment and a fine, if he causes particularly serious consequences." The infringer, in a criminal trial, faces not just the halting of their business and damage-payouts to the Seller, but imprisonment for their actions. Besides making the Seller whole again for having their business stolen, criminal sanctions are the ultimate deterrent against others in China thinking they can scam the Seller.

(II). Defense: Fighting Off Copyright Infringement Claims in China

While the media seems to only publicize the widespread copyright infringement from Chinese-nationals against American Sellers, this is not the full story. There are cases where Chinese Sellers or Chinese business have brought copyright infringement suits against Americans, Europeans and other foreigners in China who infringe upon *Chinese* products and sell them in China and abroad.

In December of 2012, a group of eight Chinese authors successfully prosecuted a copyright infringement suit against Apple.[95] Apple was found guilty by the People's Court of having violated Chinese Copyright Law by hosting third party apps that sold infringing copies of the authors' books.[96] Apple was forced to pay $165,000 to the eight authors.[97]

Sellers should notice this case and take heed, not because of the final judgement (which obviously was not very serious for Apple), but to keep in mind that this type of suit is possible. When entering the Chinese market, a seller will likely be thinking almost entirely about what to do if their copyrights are infringed. As this case highlights, however, foreign companies and foreign sellers are susceptible to claims that *they* infringed upon Chinese intellectual property rights.

---

[95] *Apple Fined By China Court for Copyright Violation*, BBC News (Dec. 28, 2012).
[96] *Id.*
[97] *Id.*

Conclusion

Copyright protections are automatic in China under the Berne Convention, but that does not mean those protections are recognized by Chinese courts. The savvy Seller will register their copyrights in order to provide more protections to products, both offensively and defensively, upon entering the Chinese marketplace. As the Chinese intellectual property landscape continues to develop and the Chinese courts become more sophisticated, the Chinese government, will likely become more willing and capable to protect its citizens' intellectual property rights. The modern-day Seller should prepared for a future where it is just as likely that their rights will be infringed upon as is that they will be accused by Chinese people and companies of infringement.

Chapter 5: Trademark: Fighting Infringers and Protecting Your Products

First and foremost, every Seller must know that China is a first-to-file country. This means that **until you register your trademark you have no rights in that trademark.**

If a Seller becomes aware that her trademarks is being infringed upon in China, the fight will center around who filed a trademark application first. The focus of protecting intellectual property rights in China must be correctly filing first.

(I). Offense: Stopping Trademark Infringers

Sellers need a Chinese-registered trademark to file a trademark infringement lawsuit in China. When issuing a complaint of trademark infringement to a Chinese online marketplace, the marketplace *requires* an approved Chinese.

There are several means by which one may seek to stop infringers and recover damages from said infringement, and we will cover the three major ways in which this can be done.

(A) Administrative Agencies

The three main administrative agencies where trademark-holders may pursue trademark infringement claims are the Administration for Industry and Commerce (AIC), the Administration of Quality Supervision, Inspection, and Quarantine (AQSIQ), and the General Administration of Customs (GAC).

The overall advantage to using an administrative agency, rather than the courts, to bring infringement claims is that it will likely act quicker less expensive. All three agencies, however, have their drawbacks as well. We will examine all three and the different aspects of their work and methods.

The Chinese AIC is a state-run agency that operates within China's provinces. It is similar in nature to the U.S. Department of Commerce. Since the AIC operates at the provincial level, it can act locally, quickly and inexpensively.[98] The AIC maintains the power to investigate trademark infringement claims and seize infringing goods.

The drawback of the AIC is, monetarily speaking, they may only award an "administrative fine" against the infringer. Generally, the administrative fine does not exceed three-times the amount of the business.[99]

---

[98] Heffels Spiegeler, *Trademark Infringement in China and the Procedure to Protect Trademarks* (Jan. 22, 2016), http://spiegeler.com/trademark-infringement-in-china-and-procedure-of-trademark-protection/.
[99] *Id.*

Second, the AQSIQ, like the AIC, can investigate, seize, and prevent the sale of infringing goods.[100] They are less-costly and work more quickly than the courts. Furthermore, because the agency is quality-focused, there is no requirement to prove trademark infringement before filing a complaint. However, and again like the AIC, they cannot issue the large damages payouts that many sellers seek when their business has been significantly harmed.

Lastly, the GAC is an administrative tool that is useful to have in any Chinese-seller's arsenal to protect their trademarks.[101] The GAC controls the border customs in China.[102] This agency can seize suspicious goods coming in and out of China regardless of whether the trademark holder has filed a complaint for trademark infringement. In order to obtain this agency's protection, a Seller need only register their trademark with Customs, and the GAC is then supposed to act on their behalf to try and protect the trademark from infringers.

(B) Civil Proceedings

The courts, like administrative agencies, may inspect, seize, and stop the sale of infringing products. They can also award much larger sums of damages than administrative agencies. Further, unlike

---

[100] Heffels Spiegeler, *Trademark Infringement in China and the Procedure to Protect Trademarks* (Jan. 22, 2016), http://spiegeler.com/trademark-infringement-in-china-and-procedure-of-trademark-protection/.

[101] General Administration of Quality Supervision, Inspection and Quarantine of P.R.C. (last visited Jun. 22, 2018), http://english.aqsiq.gov.cn/.

[102] *Id.*

administrative agencies, if a Seller receives an unfavorable ruling they may appeal to a higher court, whereas an administrative agency's decision is generally final.

Sellers seeking relief via the Chinese civil court system will issue their claim of trademark infringement to the Intellectual Property Rights Tribunal (IPR Tribunal). The IPR Tribunal will require a gathering and submission of facts from both sides and generally tries to

encourage settlement. If no settlement is reached, then the issues proceed to a trial.

(C) Criminal Proceedings

Criminal courts in China, like civil, have the benefits of being able to inspect, seize, and stop the sale of infringing goods, and issue large awards for damages. Additionally, however, the added power of a criminal case is that the infringer can be imprisoned for having infringed upon a Seller's trademark. This is a significant deterrent and an effective means of stopping an infringer.

The downsides, in addition to the cost and time of a criminal trial, is the higher-bar that a Seller must meet when alleging their products have been infringed upon. Articles 213, 214, and 215 of Chinese Criminal law indicate the standards that a plaintiff must meet in order to bring an alleged-infringer to a criminal proceeding.[103]

- Article 213: Pertains to the use of **identical marks** that requires the issue to be of a "**serious nature**" and if infringement is found, merits a punishment of "**less than 3 years**" plus fines with "**less than seven years**" for more serious crimes.[104]

- Article 214: Pertains to the use of **faked trademarks** which requires a showing that the infringer was "**knowingly selling**" infringed-products in a "**relatively large sales volume**" which merits a punishment of "**less than three years**" plus fines with "**less than seven years**" for more serious crimes.[105]

---

[103] CRIMINAL LAW OF THE PEOPLE'S REPUBLIC OF CHINA, ch. 3, § 7, art. 213-215 (Mar. 14, 1997).
[104] *Id.* art. 213.
[105] *Id.* art. 214.

- Article 215: Pertains to the use of "**[forging], selling or manufacturing**" goods without the authority of the trademark holder and the crime is "**of a serious nature**" which merits a punishment of "**less than 3 years**" plus fines with "**less than seven years**" for more serious crimes.[106]

(D) <u>Conclusion</u>

Having a trademark registration is the first step a Seller should take to protect her products in China. After this initial requirement, a Seller has many options to defend their marks. They may seek to protect their intellectual property rights through administrative agencies, civil proceedings or criminal proceedings.

(II). Defense: Fighting Off Trademark Infringement Claims

If a party in China holds a registered trademark and makes a claim that a seller's registered-trademark is infringing upon *their* mark, it is very likely that a long and arduous legal process lies ahead.

CJ's Side Note: This section sets out a very basic guide and description of how a trademark attorney, before the courts in China, would argue that your trademark is not infringing on another's mark. Please remember that, if you find yourself in this type of situation, to seek the help of experienced attorneys admitted to practice law in China.

---

[106] *Id.* art. 215.

In a trademark v. trademark battle in China where the Seller is on the defensive and being accused of infringing upon another's mark, the Seller's attorney will likely construct a multi-pronged defense. The Seller's attorney must appear before the Trademark Review Adjudication Board (TRAB) and would likely plead the following: (1) that the plaintiff's mark should not have been granted a trademark in the first place; and (2) that even if a valid trademark, the seller's mark was filed first, is from the same class, and is identical/similar.

(A) Arguing That Plaintiff Should Not Have Been Granted Trademark Protections

The means of defending a seller's trademark would be to attack the plaintiff's mark as invalid, thereby eliminating their standing in bringing the suit. A Seller's attorney will likely allege that the plaintiff's mark should be rejected on "absolute grounds" coming from Articles 10, 11, and 12 of the Trademark Law of the People's Republic of China.[107]

"Absolute grounds" for a trademark rejection means that the plaintiff's mark was inherently non-registerable due to a direct violation of one of the three articles stated above. All of the following from Article 10 will make a mark non-registerable:

> (1) Those identical with or similar to the State name, national flag, and other entities of the state;

---

[107] TRADEMARK LAW OF THE PEOPLE'S REPUBLIC OF CHINA, art. 10-12 (Aug. 30, 2013).

(2) Those identical with or similar to the State name, national flag, national emblem or military flag etc., of a foreign country, except with the consent of the government of that country;

(3) Those identical with or similar to the name, flag or emblem of an international intergovernmental organization, except with the consent of that organization or except where it is unlikely to mislead the public;

(4) Those identical with or similar to an official mark or inspection stamp that indicates control and guarantee, except where authorized;

(5) Those identical with or similar to the symbol or name of the Red Cross or the Red Crescent;

(6) Those having the nature of discrimination against any nationality;

(7) Those that are deceptive and likely to mislead the public in terms of the quality, place of production or other characteristics of the goods; and

(8) Those detrimental to socialist ethics or customs or having other unwholesome influences.[108]

If the plaintiff's mark can be revisited and rejected, then the plaintiff loses the ability to maintain her action.

---

[108] *Id.* art. 10.

The Seller's attorney may also defend the case by alleging that the plaintiff's mark violates Articles 11 or 12. Article 11 states that a mark may not be registered if the mark:

(1) Bears only the generic name, design, or model number of the goods concerned;

(2) Directly indicates the quality, principal raw materials, function, use, weight, quantity or other features of the goods; and

(3) Otherwise lacks any distinctive character.[109]

The plaintiff's mark being "generic" is a term-of-art that is similar to the same requirement under U.S. trademark law. A term is "generic" when it describes or *is* the product that it is selling. For example, "Apple" as the name for a company that sells computers and laptops, is a permissible name because it does not describe the product. Whereas "Apple" as a company that sells apples, would be generic and not permitted under either Chinese or U.S. trademark law.

An Article 12 trademark rejection applies to trademarks for three-dimensional figures that merely indicate the shape of the good being sold.

---

[109] *Id.* art. 11.

(B) The Seller's Mark was Filed First and is Similar

If the Seller's argument to reject the plaintiff's mark on "absolute grounds" is not upheld, then the second line of attack may include arguing for rejection on "relative grounds."

Because China is a first-to-file country, it is imperative that the Seller be sure that they registered their mark before the plaintiff. As Article 31 states:

Where two or more applicants apply to register identical or similar trademarks for use on the same kind of goods or similar goods, the trademark office shall first conduct examination of, give approval to and announce the trademark whose registration is applied for earlier than the rest.[110]

The first hurdle in this argument is to show that the Seller filed for their mark before the plaintiff.

After pre-filing is established, the Seller then must argue the plaintiff's mark is "identical with or similar to the trademark already registered by [the seller] or is given preliminary examination and approval for use on the same kind of goods or similar goods."[111] Under the standards set by this article, the Seller's attorney could then argue that these goods are registered for the same class of goods (which can be uncovered simply by looking at the trademark's application on the CTMO) and that the overall look and feel of the marks are substantially similar/identical.

While this stage of the argument *appears* to be simple, the ruling is left largely to the discretion of the court. As an example, "Apple" recently lost a trademark dispute in Beijing where the company tried to stop a Chinese-based maker of leather bags, belts, purses, etc. from

---

[110] *Id.* art. 31.
[111] *Id.* art. 30.

putting the term "Apple" on his products.[112] It was established that "Apple" (the American corporation) filed their trademark application several years before the alleged-infringer.[113] Despite having filed first, Apple lost the case.[114]

Anthony's Breakdown: It is important for the Seller to keep two things in mind when dealing with trademarks in China: (1) to *immediately* file when interested in a mark and (2) to keep in mind that no legal dispute has a certain outcome. The rulings by different judges in China's many different provinces may have a significant effect on arguments based upon whether two marks are truly "similar' or not to a consumer.

Conclusion

The key to successfully protecting trademarks in China, both "offensively" and "defensively" is for the Seller to file for a trademark as soon as he or she considers protecting a mark. In the event that the Seller brings a suit against an infringer, or an infringer brings a suit against the Seller alleging infringement, being able to prove the Seller were the first-to-file will greatly influence the decision maker to hold in the Seller's favor.

---

[112] Patti Waldmeir, *Apple Loses Trademark Dispute in China*, Financial Times (May 4, 2016), https://www.ft.com/content/eb72dc18-11d6-11e6-839f-2922947098f0.
[113] *Id.*
[114] *Id.*

Chapter 6: Patent: Fighting Infringers and Protecting Your Products

A patent protects novel and non-obvious innovations and inventions. In order to have protection in China, patents must be registered through SIPO. SIPO governs all patentable material in China.

Over the course of their modern development, China has quickly become the center for patent filings in the world. In 2015, China was ranked first among all nations for filings of invention patents with 1,101,864, utility model patents with 1,127,577, and design patents with 569,059. Out of these, SIPO granted 359,316 patents in 2015. The USPTO, by comparison, granted only 298,407 patents in 2015.[115]

Not only does China receive the most applications for patents, they also resolve patent issues in court faster than other countries. On average, the "time from suit filing to verdict at Beijing's IP court was 125 days. By comparison European suits take an average of 18 months. In the United States, the median time to trial in patent litigation cases is 2.4 years."[116]

---

[115] Steve Brachmann and Gene Quinn, *China Increasingly a Preferred Venue for Patent Litigation, Even for US Patent Owners*, IPWatchdog (Nov. 10, 2016), http://www.ipwatchdog.com/2016/11/10/china-increasingly-preferred-venue-patent-litigation/id=74585/.
[116] *Id.*

China employs what is essentially a first-come first-serve process when it comes to filing a patent. If there are two applications filed for the same invention or innovation, or if they are strikingly similar where only one of them should be approved, then the first application filed will have the rights to the invention.

A common strategy in China to help avoid losing the possible patent is by filing for both a utility model patent as well as an invention patent. This is done is because of the speed at which utility model patents are approved. Since both can be filed simultaneously, applicants do this and, once the utility model patent is approved, they own the idea behind it. The applicant then drops the utility model patent when the invention patent is later granted since they both cannot be running concurrently, even though they can be filed simultaneously.

There are three types of patents one can file in China: invention patents, utility model patents, and design patents.

1. Invention Patents are granted when someone invents a new technical solution, a process or the improvement thereof.[117] Invention patents are good for 20 years from the filing date. [118]
2. Utility Model Patents are granted when someone creates a new technical solutions proposed for the shape and structure of a

---

[117] PATENT LAW OF THE PEOPLE'S REPUBLIC OF CHINA, ch. V, art. 42 (2008).

[118] Id.

product, or the combination thereof, which are fit for practical use.[119] Utility Model Patents are good for 10 years from the filing date.[120]

3. Design Patents are granted when someone, with respect to a product, thinks up new designs of the shape, pattern, or the combination thereof, or the combination of the color with shape and pattern, which are rich in an aesthetic appeal and are fit for industrial application.[121] Design patents are good for 10 years from the filing date.[122]

(I). Offense: Stopping Patent Infringers

Patent infringers can come in different shapes and sizes. First, they can be someone who truly believes they own the right to the patent and they are being infringed upon. The infringer may sue the Seller based on the belief that they rightfully own the patent. The Seller will have to defend and prove that the opposite is true; that they are the true owner of the patent and they are being infringed upon.

Second, an infringer can also be someone who knows that they are infringing. These types of infringers are either trying to outright steal the Seller's product, exploit money from the Seller, or are trying to get

---

[119] PATENT LAW OF THE PEOPLE'S REPUBLIC OF CHINA, ch. I, General Provisions (2008).
[120] PATENT LAW OF THE PEOPLE'S REPUBLIC OF CHINA, ch. V, art. 42 (2008).
[121] *Id.*
[122] China IPR Help Desk, *Types of Patent in China*, Your IP Insider (Oct. 21, 2014), http://www.youripinsider.eu/types-patents-china/.

the Seller to give up their right of selling somewhere else since lawsuits to prove they are the true owner can be costly.

The most common way to stop potential infringers is to follow Article 66 of the Patent Law of the People's Republic of China, which states: "before taking legal action, file an application to request that the people's court order to have such act ceased."[123] A court order is a far cheaper and potentially less time-consuming option for any Seller looking for a quick-fix to stop an infringer. The expenses and tedium of bringing a full-blown lawsuit straight to the People's Court will save the Seller neither time nor money. The People's Court will rule within 48 hours of when it accepts the application. If they rule for the act to be ceased it will be enforced right away.[124] If the dissatisfied party files for review, the act is still the ruling of the court and will still be enforced. The applicant only has 15 days after the ruling to file a lawsuit otherwise the People's Court will withdraw their prior ruling.[125] If the applicant is mistaken, however, the applicant must compensate the other party for all losses incurred while sales were ceased during the course of the court-enforced stoppage.[126]

---

[123] PATENT LAW OF THE PEOPLE'S REPUBLIC OF CHINA, ch. V, art. 66 (2008).
[124] *Id.*
[125] Third Revision of China's Patent Law, ch. VII, art. 67 (2006 – 2008).
[126] *Id.*

Another way for Sellers with patents to make sure their rights aren't infringed upon is to follow Article 67, which outlines how to go about evidence preservation. It states that if a patent-holder is worried that "evidence might be lost or hard to acquire thereafter," then they should "file an application with the People's Court for evidence preservation."[127] By filing an application for evidence preservation, it ensures that if this case continues to trial or discovery that this information will be able to be used. The applicant does, however, need to make a guarantee, otherwise the application will be rejected. The

---

[127] PATENT LAW OF THE PEOPLE'S REPUBLIC OF CHINA, ch. VII, art. 67 (2008).

court will rule on this within 48 hours.[128] Just as article 66, if the applicant doesn't file a lawsuit within 15 days then the People's Court will withdraw their ruling.

An important caveat for Sellers is contained in Article 68. Article 68 states that the limitation for bringing an action for infringement is two years from when the patentee should have been aware or was aware of the infringement.[129] This means that the patent owner needs to keep their eyes out for anything that might be possibly infringing on their rights so that the time to bring an action, the "statute of limitations," does not expire.

There was a case in 2015 between Panasonic and two defendants who were selling products that imitated Panasonic's facial vaporizers. The patent had been issued to Panasonic in 2012. The alleged infringers started selling their products in 2013.

The defendants, Kingdom and Li Kang, were warned by Panasonic when they lodged a complaint against them to cease production and sale of said products, well within the two-year time period, as required in article 68.[130] When the defendants ignored the complaint, Panasonic

---

[128] *Id.*

[129] PATENT LAW OF THE PEOPLE'S REPUBLIC OF CHINA, ch. VII, art. 68 (2008).

[130] Sai Chen, *Determining Patent Infringement and Damages in China*, iam-media (last visited Jul. 10, 2018), http://www.iam-media.com/Intelligence/IAM-Yearbook/2018/Country-by-country/Determining-patent-infringement-and-damages-in-China.

brought a design patent infringement suit in the Beijing Intellectual Property Court.

Panasonic requested compensation of 3 million renminbi (also known as yuan or "RMB") from Kingdom, the producer of the products, and 200,000 RMB from both Kingdom and Li Kang in joint compensation.[131]

In February 2015, the Beijing court accepted the case and issued a judgement in favor of Panasonic in the amount they requested. The court also ordered the defendants to cease their actions, which violated Panasonic's patent.[132] Kingdom and Li Kang's appeal failed. The compensatory award was upheld.[133]

This monetary ruling was extremely unprecedented. Article 65 of the Patent Law of the People's Republic of China states the range of compensation should fall from 10,000 renminbi to 1,000,000 renminbi.[134] The damages achieved in this case fall far outside the usual six-figure norm. This case indicates a significant shift in the patent laws in China and a sign to Sellers seeking to protect their patents in China will be treated more fairly than ever before.

---

[131] *Id.*
[132] *Id.*
[133] *Id.*
[134] *Id.*

(II). Defense: Defending Patent Infringement Claims

If someone is suing a patent-holding Seller under a false claim that the Seller is infringing on *his or her* patents, there are many defenses a Seller can assert. Below are several of the most common allegations asserted and common defenses Sellers may raise.

(A) Non-Patentable Subject Matter

Article 25 of the Patent Law of the People's Republic of China, prohibits patents being granted for:

> (1) Scientific discoveries;
>
> (2) Rules and methods for intellectual activities;
>
> (3) Methods for the diagnosis or treatment of diseases;
>
> (4) Animal or plant varieties;
>
> (5) Substances obtained by means of nuclear transformation; and
>
> (6) Designs that are mainly used for marking the pattern, color or the combination of the two of prints.[135]

Patent holders are subject to losing their patent if it was improperly granted. A patent that was granted in violation of any of the six categories may be lost if challenged.

---

[135] PATENT LAW OF THE PEOPLE'S REPUBLIC OF CHINA, ch. II, art. 25 (2008).

(B) Harmful to the Public Interest

There are guidelines as to what is not patentable under Article 5:

"Patent rights shall not be granted for invention-creations that violate the law or social ethics, or harm public interests. Patent rights shall not be granted for inventions that are accomplished by relying on genetic resources which are obtained or used in violation of the provisions of laws and administrative regulations."

These restrictions are vague when compared to the provisions in Article 25. This gives the SIPO discretion granting patents or refusing them. If the Court, for example, decides that the patent "harms public interest," SIPO can refuse the patent or vacate it.

(C) Prior Use

A Seller can defend herself in a patent claim via arguing "prior use." "Prior Use" is when someone was using the invention or innovation before the patent application was filed. The Seller would argue that she has been using this patented invention before it was even filed for protection This issue is discussed in the Patent Laws at Article 69 (2).

(D) Prior Art

A Seller can respond to an infringement claim via arguing "prior art" defense. Prior Art means that the product has been published somewhere in the world before the Chinese patent filing date.[136]

Because of the first-to-file system, a foreign applicant needs to keep their future invention a secret, otherwise their patent might not be approved. If the future patented product is well-known art or technology, and is identifiable, then future opposition can bring that argument to invalidate the Seller's patent.

(E) Invalidation of Patent

Those alleging infringement against a Seller will likely seek to invalidate the Seller's patent. If that goal is achieved, then there is essentially nothing to infringe upon, and the individual would be free to

---

[136] Alex Zhang, *Key Considerations for Patent Strategies in China*, IP (Nov. 26, 2011), http://www.ipwatchdog.com/2011/11/06/key-considerations-for-patent-strategies-in-china/id=20241/.

create/use the once patented material as they wish. This is a strategy that Sellers can also use against their accusers.

When seeking to invalidate a patent, a claim must be brought before the Patent Re-examination Board ("PRB").[137] The PRB takes about 6 months to rule if the patent is either validated wholly, invalidated, or partially invalidated. Each party then has three months to appeal the decision. If the parties patent is ruled invalid and is upheld as such in the Beijing Intermediate People's Court, on appeal, then the claim for infringement will be dismissed.

In 2012 Xima Co., a Chinese company, attempted to invalidate Kohler's design patents for the NUMI toilet, which had won numerous awards.[138] Kohler filed an infringement lawsuit against Xima after repeated warnings. In response, Xima filed requests for invalidation against Kohler's design patents. Xima tried three times to invalidate Kohler's patent and was successful. Kohler then filed an administrative lawsuit seeking a reversal of Xima's successful claim.[139] The Beijing IP Court upheld Kohler's patent and revoked the decision by the PRB.[140] As of the date of the publication of this book, Xima is appealing the decision.

---

[137] PATENT LAW OF THE PEOPLE'S REPUBLIC OF CHINA, ch. V, art. 45 (2008).
[138] *Strategies for Patentee Lawsuits Against Design Invalidations*, China Business Law Journal (Oct. 9. 2017), https://www.vantageasia.com/strategies-patentee-lawsuits-design-invalidations/.
[139] *Id.*
[140] *Id.*

Pfizer was compelled to appeal a lower court's decision to invalidate their patent in 2004. Pfizer filed for a Chinese patent for Viagra in May of 1994. The SIPO granted the patent in 2001.[141] Twelve domestic Chinese drug companies challenged the patent since they claimed they had already invested upwards of $12 million into producing similar generic versions of the drug. SIPO's Patent Re-examination Board invalidated Pfizer's patent in July of 2004, based on a claimed lack of data in the application filed by Pfizer to support Viagra's therapeutic effects.[142] Pfizer appealed the decision to invalidate its patent and brought the issue to the Beijing Intermediate People's Court.

In June 2006, the Beijing court agreed with Pfizer. This decision was appealed again by the Chinese manufacturers to the Beijing Higher People's Court. The High Court rejected the appeal and reaffirmed that Pfizer owned the Viagra Patent.

> **CJ's Tip:** Viagra is important to all Sellers two reasons…that do not relate to consuming Viagra. First, businesses in China attack patents that clearly belong to others. Second, U.S. companies can protect themselves and their intellectual property rights in China.

---

[141] *Id.*
[142] *Id.*

Chapter 7: Trade Dress: Fighting Infringers and Protecting Your Products

Trade Dress refers to non-functional (non-essential for the item's use or quality), distinctive (either inherently or through acquired secondary meaning); and the overall shape, color, texture and design of a product and its packaging.

There are no specific trade dress laws in China. Sellers cannot rely upon trade dress intellectual property rights to protect their products in China.

Trade Dress solely exists in China as a facet of other established intellectual property rights. Trade Dress, arguably, stems from China's Anti-Unfair Competition Law (AUCL).[143] Trade Dress protections can be protected in China, in part, via utilizing China's copyright, trademark, and patent infringement laws.

(I). Offense: Stopping Trade Dress Infringers

(A) Copyright

As discussed in Chapter 3, copyright protections are automatic in China but may also be registered for either domestically or internationally via the Madrid Protocol.

---

[143] *See generally* LAW OF THE PEOPLE'S REPUBLIC OF CHINA AGAINST UNFAIR COMPETITION (last visited Jun. 27, 2018), http://www.wipo.int/edocs/lexdocs/laws/en/cn/cn011en.pdf.

Historically, copyright protections for foreign Sellers, companies, and corporations in China have been notoriously weak. In recent years, however, the People's Court has issued rulings that seem to be changing the tide in China pertaining to an increased recognition of "trade dress".

In 2017, the People's Court issued a ruling in favor of Lego, the world's most profitable toy company in 2013[144] and manufacturer of the popular children's building-block toys.

The toy industry in China is estimated to be worth $31 billion.[145]

After Lego brought suit in China, the China Shantou Intermediate People's Court ruled that "certain Bela products infringed upon the copyrights of the Lego Group and that manufacturing and selling of those products constituted acts of unfair competition."[146] The Court went on to say that certain products were protected under the AUCL.[147] The trade dress of Lego's products had "the distinctive and unique appearance of certain decorative aspects of its packaging across

---

[144] Tom Metcalf and Robert LaFranco, *Lego Builds New Billionaires as Toymaker Topple Mattel*, Bloomberg (Mar. 13, 2013), https://www.bloomberg.com/news/articles/2013-03-13/lego-builds-new-billionaires-as-toymaker-topples-mattel.

[145] *Toymaker Wins Lego Chinese Copyright Case Against Brick Imitators*, Reuters (Dec. 7, 2017), https://www.reuters.com/article/us-lego-china-copyright/toymaker-lego-wins-chinese-copyright-case-against-brick-imitators-idUSKBN1E1157.

[146] *Id.*

[147] *Id.*

particular product lines."[148] As a result, Bela could no longer copy these unique trade dress aspects.

(B) Trademark

Trade Dress has been successfully protected in China via bringing suit under China's trademark laws.

Both STIHL, the chainsaw manufacturer, and Activision Blizzard, the creators of the popular online game *World of Warcraft*, won trademark lawsuits in China where the issue of trade dress infringement was raised.

In STIHL, a Hangzhou machinery company manufactured chainsaws with Stihl's color scheme.[149] STIHL was deemed by the court to have trade dress protection for its distinctive orange-and gray color scheme.

Activision Blizzard brought an action against a Chinese company for publishing an infringing game called *Everyone WarCraft: War of Draenor*. The Chinese company had copied much of World of

---

[148] *Id.*

[149] Wanhuida Peksung, *STIHL's Color Combination Trade Dress Obtains Judicial Protection in China*, Lexology (Feb. 14, 2016), https://www.lexology.com/library/detail.aspx?g=6a580270-1e3f-4482-b7df-3b84457e089e.

Warcraft's look and feel.[150] Activision Blizzard was awarded trade dress protection for the look and feel of *World of Warcraft*, including such elements as character names and designs, equipment icons, maps, and game interface.[151]

Besides being able to more frequently raise trade dress claims during trademark infringement suits, in 2008, China saw one of the first lawsuits where a plaintiff raised a claim entirely based upon infringement of trade dress rights under the AUCL. Ferrero Rocher

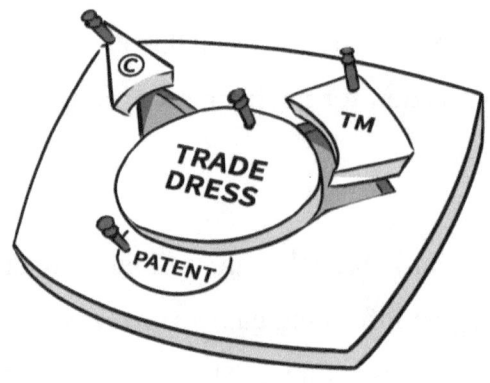

[150] Shanghai Patent & Trademark Office, LLC, *World of Warcraft Prevails In First-Instance of Copyright Infringement and Unfair Competition Dispute* (last visited Jul. 9, 2018), http://www.sptl.com/newsitem/277585792.
[151] *Id.*

brought suit in the People's Court against a company that mimicked the gold-colored foil packaging around their famed hazelnut-centered chocolates.

Montresor had created virtually identical chocolates.[152]

Despite being "known" for their packaging, Ferrero Rocher could not bring a trademark infringement claim because it had failed to register its mark in China. Instead, Ferrero Rocher brought the suit under China's AUCL.

The AUCL states that a party must not, without the consent of the manufacturer of "well-known merchandise," use packing or decoration that is identical or similar to the unique packaging or decoration of "well-known merchandise." This creates confusion among consumers that its products are the "well-known merchandise."

The Chinese Supreme Court affirmation marked a distinct advancement in the development of trade dress law in China.

Anthony's Advice: The Chinese Court's increasing acceptance of trade dress as a viable intellectual property right is great news

---

[152] Fiona Tam, *Italian Chocolate Firm Ferro Wins Court Battle Against China Fakes*, South China Morning Post (Apr. 9, 2008), https://www.scmp.com/article/633067/italian-chocolate-firm-ferrero-wins-court-battle-against-china-fakes.

for sellers. As it still stands, however, Sellers should treat trade dress as a very new intellectual property right in China that they may or may not be able to raise. It should not be seen as a substitute for a properly registered copyright or trademark, but rather a supplement.

(II). Defense: Defending Trade Dress Infringement Claims

In China, trade dress is neither well defined nor given any specific protections.[153] As the *Ferrero* case explained, a trade dress infringement claim can only be brought if the product being infringed upon is "well-known merchandise."[154] Therefore, an individual or company seeking to raise a trade dress infringement claim against a seller must prove that their merchandise is so "well known," and the Seller's products are so identical that the Seller infringed upon their trade dress.

Sellers seeking to avoid this type of lawsuit in China simply needs to not mimic a Chinese company's products. Not copying another company's products is sound advice, not just in the Chinese market, but around the world.

---

[153] Frost, Brown, Todd LLC, *China's Supreme Court Sides With Foreign Owner Of Famous Consumer Product, Despite Lack Of Trademark Protection* (Jun. 23, 2008), https://www.frostbrowntodd.com/resources-06-23-2008.html.
[154] *Id.*

Conclusion

Trade dress is the least recognized and most ill-defined intellectual property right in China. Sellers should not rely on trade dress to protect their products. However, trade dress is appearing more frequently as a feature of more recognizable intellectual property lawsuits in China, such as copyright infringement and trademark infringement cases. Sellers should work to ensure that their products neither infringe upon the originality of another's design nor are likely to confuse consumers as to the origins of a product.

Chapter 8: The Final Comments on Intellectual Property in China

(I).   A Review of the Main Topics

(A) History of Intellectual Property in China

China's current intellectual property laws are all relatively new even though China's historic protections date back to 835 A.D. when the China's first copyright regulation was instituted.

Trademark protections in China began during the Tang Dynasty (618-907 A.D.) when trade was flourishing and distinction between goods became a necessity.[155] This blossomed into a fully-fledged system during the Ming Dynasty (1368- 1644 A.D.) when registering trademarks between guilds was common.[156]

In 1979, China joined the world of intellectual property and signed a bilateral agreement with the United States to allow for protection of American copyrights, patents and trademarks in China. China joined the Berne Convention, the World Intellectual Property Organization, the Paris Convention, and the Patent Cooperation Treaty; all organizations interested in the furtherance of intellectual property rights. China's internal organization for intellectual property protections

---

[155] Hamideh Ramjerdi & Anthony D'Amato, *The Intellectual Property Rights Laws of The People's Republic of China*, 21 N.C.J. Int'l L. & Com. Reg. 169, 172 (1995).
[156] Charles Baum, *Trade Sanctions and the Rule of Law: Lessons from China*, Stan. J. E. Asian Aff. 46, 51 (2001),
http://www.stanford.edu/group/sjeaa/journal/china4.pdf.

are the State Intellectual Property Organization and the Chinese Trademark Office.

(B) Registering for Intellectual Property Protection in China

Regardless of Seller's intellectual property protections in the United States, Sellers should register their rights in China. Without

formal protection under the intellectual property organizations in China, a Seller being sued for infringement or trying to get another to stop selling a product that closely resembles his or hers may have no redress without filing in China.

(C) Copyright

Since China is member of the Berne Convention, Sellers automatically have copyright protection in China… although these may not be recognized by Chinese courts. When Sellers' copyright protections arise solely from the Berne Convention's automatic protection copyright protections, it likely will not be enough to defend the works in the Chinese court system. Sellers should register their rights in China.

The easiest way to register for copyright in China is through the Copyright Protection Center of China. Follow the steps one-by-one. Sellers can gain copyright for their product in China.

Copyrights in China are protected for the life of the author plus 70 years after death. The cheapest way to deal with an infringer is to first contact the selling-website and inform them of the existing copyright and ask the infringing product to be removed. Products can also be protected through a series of increasingly effective but costly systems such as: registering the copyrights with the Regulations on Customs Protection of Intellectual Property Rights, seeking administrative proceedings to stop local-level infringers, or by bringing a civil or criminal suit in the People's Court. The Chinese have the power to preserve the infringing material, so the infringer cannot hide it or destroy it if they are caught. The most important power the courts have for the Seller is they can award damages, which technically have no limit, even though courts tend to award less than the damaged party requested.

(D) Trademark

The two possible ways to register for trademark protection is either through the Madrid Protocol or with the Chinese Trademark Office (CTMO). The Madrid Protocol is a user-friendly process in which one can protect their product in multiple countries (about 100) via one simple application.

The issue with the Madrid Protocol, however, is that an applicant who files with WIPO in turn, has the application sent to the CTMO. There is an 11-month period in which the CTMO reviews the application and only after will the applicant find out whether their application was approved or denied. If the applicant decides to file directly with the CTMO it is faster.

Chinese trademarks operate on a first-to-file system. Sellers seeking to protect their mark in China, *must* register their marks in China. I

Sellers have multiple options in China to protect their rights including:

- Assistance from the Administration for Industry and Commerce (AIC),

- The Administration of Quality Supervision, Inspection, and Quarantine, and;
- The General Administration of Customs (GAC), or the civil and criminal courts overseen by the IPR Tribunal.

Sellers being sued for trademark infringement should seek legal assistance and have multiple defenses that can be asserted including:

- The Sellers filed-first, or
- The opposing party's trademark is invalid as it falls under Articles 10, 11, or 12 of the Trademark Law of the People's Republic of China.

(E) Patent

For patent protection, Sellers should for protection with China's State Intellectual Property Office of the People's Republic of China (SIPO).

There is no international agreement for patent protection in China. Sellers must file with the SIPO even if they have a patent elsewhere.

China is the patent-filing hub of the world. Applications can be highly complex and can only be filed in Mandarin. China employs a first-come first-serve process. The first patent application filed in the system will be examined first and could potentially invalidate later patents that appear strikingly similar. Patent litigation, both offensively and defensively, is a complex process and Sellers experiencing issues should hire an experienced Chinese attorney.

(F) Trade Dress

Trade Dress is slowly beginning to be recognized by the courts in China. Trade dress in China, at the very most, should be seen by the seller as another argument to be made in a pre-existing intellectual property lawsuit to protect their product.

(II). Final Words

Interaction with the Chinese market, in terms of sales or manufacturing, requires vigilance to identify infringement and defend products and brands. If there are issues with your products or brands, there are numerous routes available for redress.

TABLE OF AUTHORITIES

- 15 U.S.C. § 1127.

- *About Customs Enforcement of Intellectual Property Right (IPR)*, General Administration of Customs People's Republic of China (Nov. 18, 2014), http://english.customs.gov.cn/Statics/aafe7743-c701-4795-91e3-6f3fdf7ce397.html.

- AFD China Intellectual Property Law Office, *China's Trademark Application Amounts to 3.691 Million in 2016* (Mar. 2017), https://www.lexology.com/library/detail.aspx?g=e81f8156-da99-435f-8cdc-5ee6fbe6865f.

- Alex Zhang, *Key Considerations for Patent Strategies in China*, IP (Nov. 26, 2011), http://www.ipwatchdog.com/2011/11/06/key-considerations-for-patent-strategies-in-china/id=20241/.

- *Apple Fined By China Court for Copyright Violation*, BBC News (Dec. 28, 2012).

- *Best Practices: Intellectual Property Protection in China*, The US-China Business Council (2015), https://www.uschina.org/reports/best-practices-intellectual-property-protection-china.

- Charles Baum, *Trade Sanctions and the Rule of Law: Lessons from China*, Stan. J. E. Asian Aff. 46, 51 (2001), http://www.stanford.edu/group/sjeaa/journal/china4.pdf.

- China IPR Help Desk, *Types of Patent in China*, Your IP Insider (Oct. 21, 2014), http://www.youripinsider.eu/types-patents-china/.

- *China Laws (302 texts)*, WIPO World Intellectual Property Organization (last visited Jun. 18, 2018), http://www.wipo.int/wipolex/en/profile.jsp?code=cn.

- *China Uncovers Almost 1,600 U.S.-Related Intellectual Property Infringements This Year*, Reuters (Nov. 8, 2017), https://www.reuters.com/article/us-china-u-s-intellectual-property/china-uncovers-almost-1600-u-s-related-intellectual-property-infringements-this-year-idUSKBN1D90A0.

- *China's Long and Tortured History*, JIPEL Blog (Feb. 4, 2014), https://blog.jipel.law.nyu.edu/2014/02/chinas-long-and-tortured-history-when-it-comes-to-intellectual-property-laws/.

- Christopher Beam, *Bootleg Nation*, Slate (Oct. 22, 2009), http://www.slate.com/articles/news_and_politics/explainer/2009/10/bootleg_nation.html.

- CJ Rosenbaum, *Your Guide to Amazon Suspensions* (2017-2018 ed.).

- Clare Sebastian, *Chinese Trade Secret Theft Nearly Killed Company,* CNN tech (Mar. 23, 2018), http://money.cnn.com/2018/03/23/technology/business/american-semiconductor-china-trade/index.html.

- COPYRIGHT LAW OF THE PEOPLE'S REPUBLIC OF CHINA, art. 21, § 3 (Feb. 26, 2010).

- COPYRIGHT LAW OF THE PEOPLE'S REPUBLIC OF CHINA, art. 21, § 3 (Feb. 26, 2010).

- COPYRIGHT LAW OF THE PEOPLE'S REPUBLIC OF CHINA, art. 22, § 4 (Feb. 26, 2010).

- COPYRIGHT LAW OF THE PEOPLE'S REPUBLIC OF CHINA, art. 3.

- COPYRIGHT LAW OF THE UNITED STATES, ch. 3, § 301(a), (Dec. 2016).

- Copyright Protection Center of China (last visited Jun. 19, 2018), http://www.ccopyright.com/.

- CRIMINAL LAW OF THE PEOPLE'S REPUBLIC OF CHINA, art. 217, § 7 (Mar. 14, 1997).

- CRIMINAL LAW OF THE PEOPLE'S REPUBLIC OF CHINA, ch. 3, § 7, art. 213-215 (Mar. 14, 1997).

- Crystal J. Chen, Eric C. K. Hsieh, and Sylvester W. L. Hsieh, China: Managing the IP Lifecycle 2013 *The Patent Application Process Explained*, iam-media (last visited July 16, 2018), http://www.iam-media.com/Intelligence/IP-Lifecycle-China/2013/Articles/The-patent-application-process-explained.

- Dennis C. Blair and Keith Alexander, *China's Intellectual Property Theft Must Stop*, NY Times (Aug. 15, 2017), https://www.nytimes.com/2017/08/15/opinion/china-us-intellectual-property-trump.html.

- *File: Madrid e-Services*, WIPO World Intellectual Property Organization (last visited Jun. 19, 2018), http://www.wipo.int/madrid/en/file/.

- Fiona Tam, *Italian Chocolate Firm Ferro Wins Court Battle Against China Fakes*, South China Morning Post (Apr. 9, 2008), https://www.scmp.com/article/633067/italian-chocolate-firm-ferrero-wins-court-battle-against-china-fakes.

- Frost, Brown, Todd LLC, *China's Supreme Court Sides With Foreign Owner Of Famous Consumer Product, Despite Lack Of Trademark Protection* (Jun. 23, 2008), https://www.frostbrowntodd.com/resources-06-23-2008.html.

- General Administration of Quality Supervision, Inspection and Quarantine of P.R.C. (last visited Jun. 22, 2018), http://english.aqsiq.gov.cn/.

- *Global Brand Database,* WIPO World Intellectual Property Organization (last visited Jun. 19, 2018), http://www.wipo.int/branddb/en/.

- *Guide To Patent Protection In China*, China IPR SME Helpdesk (2013), http://www.china-iprhelpdesk.eu/sites/all/docs/publications/China_IPR_Guide-Guide_to_Patent_Protection_in_China_EN-2013.pdf.

- Hamideh Ramjerdi & Anthony D'Amato, *The Intellectual Property Rights Laws of The People's Republic of China*, 21 N.C.J. Int'l L. & Com. Reg. 169, 172 (1995).

- Heffels Spiegeler, *Trademark Infringement in China and the Procedure to Protect Trademarks* (Jan. 22, 2016), http://spiegeler.com/trademark-infringement-in-china-and-procedure-of-trademark-protection/.

- *How To File A Copyright Registration In China*, China IPR (2018), http://www.china-iprhelpdesk.eu/sites/china-hd/files/public/v8_How_to_Register_Copyright.pdf.

- *International Registration of Marks – Fee Calculation*, WIPO World Intellectual Property Organization (last visited Jun. 19, 2018), http://www.wipo.int/madrid/en/fees/calculator.jsp.

- Jeff Mason, *Exclusive: Trump Considers Big 'Fine' Over China Intellectual Property Theft*, Reuters (Jan. 17, 2018), https://www.reuters.com/article/us-usa-trump-trade-exclusive/exclusive-trump-considers-big-fine-over-china-intellectual-property-theft-idUSKBN1F62SR.

- LAW OF THE PEOPLE'S REPUBLIC OF CHINA AGAINST UNFAIR COMPETITION, art. 10, § 3 (Dec. 1, 1993).

- *Madrid Monitor*, WIPO World Intellectual Property Organization (last visited Jun. 19, 2018), http://www.wipo.int/madrid/monitor/en/index.jsp.

- Matt Slater, *List of Chinese AIC Websites*, China Checkup (Oct. 15, 2013), https://www.chinacheckup.com/blogs/articles/chinese-aic-websites-list.

- Matthew Dresden, *China Copyright Law: We Need to Talk*, China Law Blog (Oct. 17, 2016), https://www.chinalawblog.com/2016/10/china-copyright-law-we-need-to-talk.html.

- Matthew Dresden, *China Trademarks, The Madrid System, And Star Trek*, China Law Blog (Jul. 10, 2016), https://www.chinalawblog.com/2016/07/china-trademarks-the-madrid-system-and-star-trek.html.

- Nicholas Mortl and Derek Turhan, *Seller's Guide to Brand Protection*, ch. 5, Amazon Tools, Brand Gating.

- Office of the United States Trade Representative, 2017 Special 301 Report (last visited Mar. 25, 2017), https://ustr.gov/sites/default/files/301/2017%20Special%20301%20Report%20FINAL.PDF.

- Office of the United States Trade Representative, 2017 Special 301 Report (last visited Mar. 25, 2017), https://ustr.gov/sites/default/files/301/2017%20Special%20301%20Report%20FINAL.PDF.

- PATENT LAW OF THE PEOPLE'S REPUBLIC OF CHINA, ch. I, General Provisions (2008).

- PATENT LAW OF THE PEOPLE'S REPUBLIC OF CHINA, ch. II, art. 25 (2008).

- PATENT LAW OF THE PEOPLE'S REPUBLIC OF CHINA, ch. V, art. 42 (2008).

- PATENT LAW OF THE PEOPLE'S REPUBLIC OF CHINA, ch. V, art. 45 (2008).

- PATENT LAW OF THE PEOPLE'S REPUBLIC OF CHINA, ch. V, art. 66 (2008).

- PATENT LAW OF THE PEOPLE'S REPUBLIC OF CHINA, ch. VII, art. 67 (2008).

- PATENT LAW OF THE PEOPLE'S REPUBLIC OF CHINA, ch. VII, art. 68 (2008).

- Patti Waldmeir, *Apple Loses Trademark Dispute in China*, Financial Times (May 4, 2016), https://www.ft.com/content/eb72dc18-11d6-11e6-839f-2922947098f0.

- *Protecting Your Inventions Abroad: Frequently Asked Questions About The Patent Cooperation Treaty (PCT)*, WIPO World Intellectual Property Organization (status on Oct 2017).

- Qiao Dexi *A Survey Of Intellectual Property Issues In China-U.S. Trade Negotiations Under The Special 301 Provisions*, Pacific Rim Law & Policy Journal Vol. 2 No. 2, 259, 260.

- Ran Wang and Xiaojing Wang, *Protecting Trade Secrets In China*, Managing Intellectual Property (Sept. 06, 2017), http://www.managingip.com/Article/3748735/Protecting-trade-secrets-in-China.html.

- Regulations on Customs Protection of Intellectual Property Rights, Decree No. 395 of State Council of the People's Republic of China (effective Mar. 1, 2004).

- *Roadmap for Intellectual Property Protection in China*, EU-China IPR2, 16.

- Sai Chen, *Determining Patent Infringement and Damages in China*, iam-media (last visited Jul. 10, 2018), http://www.iam-media.com/Intelligence/IAM-Yearbook/2018/Country-by-country/Determining-patent-infringement-and-damages-in-China.

- *See* Appistry, Inc. v. Amazon.com, Inc., No. C15-311 MJP, 2015 U.S. Dist. LEXIS 90004 (W.D. Wash. July 9, 2015) (where Amazon successfully showed the patents were invalid).

- *See generally,* LAW OF THE PEOPLE'S REPUBLIC OF CHINA AGAINST UNFAIR COMPETITION (last visited Jun. 27, 2018), http://www.wipo.int/edocs/lexdocs/laws/en/cn/cn011en.pdf.

- Shanghai Patent & Trademark Office, LLC, *World of Warcraft Prevails In First-Instance of Copyright Infringement and Unfair Competition Dispute* (last visited Jul. 9, 2018), http://www.sptl.com/newsitem/277585792.

- Staff Editor, *China's Long and Tortured History When It Comes To Intellectual Property Laws*, JIPEL Blog – NYU Journal of Intellectual Property & Entertainment Law (Feb. 4, 2014), https://blog.jipel.law.nyu.edu/2014/02/chinas-long-and-tortured-history-when-it-comes-to-intellectual-property-laws/.

- State Intellectual Property Office, SIPO.gov (last visited Jun. 19, 18), http://english.sipo.gov.cn/.

- Steve Brachmann and Gene Quinn, *China Increasingly a Preferred Venue for Patent Litigation, Even for US Patent Owners*, IPWatchdog (Nov. 10, 2016), http://www.ipwatchdog.com/2016/11/10/china-increasingly-preferred-venue-patent-litigation/id=74585/.

- *Strategies for Patentee Lawsuits Against Design Invalidations*, China Business Law Journal (Oct. 9. 2017), https://www.vantageasia.com/strategies-patentee-lawsuits-design-invalidations/.

- *Summary of Madrid Agreement Concerning the International*, WIPO World Intellectual Property Organization (last visited Jun. 19, 2018), http://www.wipo.int/treaties/en/registration/madrid/summary_madrid_marks.html.

- *Summary of the Paris Convention for the Protection of Industrial Property (1883)*, WIPO World Intellectual Property Organization (last visited Jun. 22, 2018).

- Supreme People's Court, *China's Intellectual Property Judicial Protection Program (2016-2020)*, law-lib.com (last visited Jun. 18, 2018), http://www.law-lib.com/law/law_view.asp?id=566119.

- Third Revision of China's Patent Law, ch. VII, art. 67 (2006 – 2008).

- Tom Metcalf and Robert LaFranco, *Lego Builds New Billionaires as Toymaker Topple Mattel*, Bloomberg (Mar. 13, 2013), https://www.bloomberg.com/news/articles/2013-03-13/lego-builds-new-billionaires-as-toymaker-topples-mattel.

- *Toymaker Wins Lego Chinese Copyright Case Against Brick Imitators*, Reuters (Dec. 7, 2017), https://www.reuters.com/article/us-lego-china-copyright/toymaker-lego-wins-chinese-copyright-case-against-brick-imitators-idUSKBN1E1157.

- Trade Dress, law.cornell.edu (last visited Jun. 19, 2018), https://www.law.cornell.edu/wex/trade_dress.

- *Trademark Classifications List of Goods and Services*, Chinese Trademark Office (last visited Jun. 19, 2018), https://www.chinatrademarkoffice.com/blog/show/190.html.

- TRADEMARK LAW OF THE PEOPLE'S REPUBLIC OF CHINA, art. 10-12 (Aug. 30, 2013).

- TRADEMARK LAW OF THE PEOPLE'S REPUBLIC OF CHINA, ch. II, art. 10 (Aug. 30, 2013).

- TRADEMARK LAW OF THE PEOPLE'S REPUBLIC OF CHINA, ch. II, art. 19 (Aug. 30, 2013).

- TRADEMARK LAW OF THE PEOPLE'S REPUBLIC OF CHINA, ch. II, art. 24 – ch. III, art. 30.

- U.S. Const. art. I, § 8.

- *U.S. Relations With China 1949-2018,* cfr.org (last visited Jun. 18, 2018), https://www.cfr.org/timeline/us-relations-china.

- Wang Lewei, *The Chinese Traditions Inimical to Patent Law*, 14 NW. J. Int'l & Bus. 15, 36-56(1993).

- Wang Ze, Zhou Yunchuan, Zhou Bo, Rui Songyan and Xu Lin, Landmark Trademark Cases in China: An In-Depth Analysis, 61.

- Wanhuida Peksung, *How to File? Directly in China with the CTMO or Through International Extension to China?*, Wan Hu Dai Intellectual Property Express, No. 32 (Jul. 2016 Issue), http://www.managingip.com/Article/3669018/How-to-file-Directly-in-China-with-the-CTMO-or-through-international-extension-to-China.html.

- Wanhuida Peksung, *STIHL's Color Combination Trade Dress Obtains Judicial Protection in China*, Lexology (Feb. 14, 2016), https://www.lexology.com/library/detail.aspx?g=6a580270-1e3f-4482-b7df-3b84457e089e.

- Wei Shei, *Cultural Perplexity in Intellectual Property: Is Stealing a Book an Elegant Offense*, 32 N.C.J. Int'l L. & Com. Reg. 1 (2006); *quoting* John R. Allison & Lianlian Lin, *The Evolution of Chinese Attitudes toward Property Rights Invention and Discovery*, 20 U. Pa. J. Int'l Econ. L. 735, 744 (1999).

- WIPO World Intellectual Property Organization, (last visited Jun. 19, 2018), http://www.wipo.int/about-ip/en/.

- WIPO World Intellectual Property Organization, *China Tops Patent, Trademark, Design Filings in 2016* (Dec. 6, 2017), http://www.wipo.int/pressroom/en/articles/2017/article_0013.h tml.

- *WIPO-Administered Treaties*, WIPO World Intellectual Property Organization (last visited Jun. 19, 2018), http://www.wipo.int/treaties/en/ShowResults.jsp?treaty_id=15.
- Xuri Bao, *China: Strengthening Trade Dress Protection In China*, World Trademark Review (May 01, 2017), http://www.worldtrademarkreview.com/Magazine/Issue/67/Co untry-correspondents/Strengthening-trade-dress-protection-in-China.

www.ingramcontent.com/pod-product-compliance
Lightning Source LLC
Chambersburg PA
CBHW030818180526
45163CB00003B/1339